LOVE
the PSYCHOLOGY of ATTRACTION

LESLIE BECKER-PHELPS Ph.D.

WITH MEGAN KAYE

Writer Megan Kaye
Senior Editor Camilla Hallinan
Senior Art Editor Karen Constanti
Illustrator Keith Hagan
Design and Illustration Assistant Laura Buscemi
Senior Jacket Creative Nicola Powling
Producer, Pre-Production Dragana Puvacic
Senior Producer Jen Scothern
Creative Technical Support
Sonia Charbonnier
Managing Editor Dawn Henderson
Managing Art Editor Christine Keilty
Art Directors Peter Luff, Maxine Pedliham
Publisher Peggy Vance

First published in Great Britain in 2016
by Dorling Kindersley Limited
80 Strand, London WC2R 0RL
A Penguin Random House Company

A CIP catalogue record for this book is
available from the British Library
ISBN 978 0 2411 8227 7

Colour reproduction by Altaimage UK
Printed and bound in China

All images © Dorling Kindersley Limited
For further information see: www.dkimages.com

A WORLD OF IDEAS:
SEE ALL THERE IS TO KNOW

Consultant psychologist:
Leslie Becker-Phelps Ph.D.

Dr Becker-Phelps is a clinical psychologist,
author, and speaker. She is a regular contributor
to the *Relationships* blog for WebMD, as well as
the *Making Changes* blog for *Psychology Today*,
and is the author of *Insecure in Love* (2014).
She lives in New Jersey, USA, where she is on
the medical staff of the Robert Wood Johnson
University Hospital Somerset. She also runs
a private practice dedicated to helping
individuals and couples feel better about
themselves in all aspects of their lives.

ACKNOWLEDGMENTS

Leslie Becker-Phelps:
This book was truly a collaborative project. I'm greatly
appreciative of everyone's efforts: the theorists and
researchers whose work we are sharing; the many
colleagues in the New Jersey Psychological Association
who were always ready to share their expertise along the
way; Kathy Cortese, Eileen Kennedy Moore, and Shari
Kuchenbecker for their friendship and collegial support;
Megan Kaye and Camilla Hallinan for their editorial
expertise; and finally my husband, Mark, for his support in
this and in everything that I do.

The publisher would like to thank:
Philip R. Shaver Ph.D., Distinguished Professor of
Psychology at UC Davis, for his kind permission to
include the "Love Quiz", devised wth Cindy Hazan
and first published in the *Rocky Mountain News* in
1987; Rita Carter, Anna Davidson, Dr Sue Johnson,
and Bob Saxton for their insightful comments during the
creation of this book; Jennifer Latham for proofreading;
Helen Peters for the index; Mandy Earey and Anne Fisher
for design help; and US editor Kate Johnsen.

CONTENTS

CHAPTER 3
DATING
MAKING IT WORK

CHAPTER 4
ESTABLISHING
THE
RELATIONSHIP
FROM ATTRACTION TO COMMITMENT

FOREWORD

Everyone yearns for that magical feeling of being in love. But falling for someone is just the start: what we need most is an emotionally nourishing, caring relationship. That's what we dream of, deep down – not just a partner, but a soul mate. Sometimes, if we've been single for a long time, we can start to wonder whether we should just give up – we may even feel embarrassed for wanting romance as much as we do. If you've ever felt that way, I want you to know that by yearning for a relationship, you're simply feeling the way that nature intended. The science suggests that we're born to be social creatures, deeply connected to those around us. As children, we bond passionately with our parents or caregivers; as adults, that need matures and transforms. We become filled with the desire for romantic love. Love may not always be easy to find, but it is literally the most natural thing in the world to want.

More than twenty years as a therapist have confirmed for me a simple insight: that when we can give and receive love whole-heartedly, we are at our strongest. The psychological community as a whole is finding more and more empirical evidence – from decades of in-depth studies to the latest brain imaging techniques – that we are biologically predisposed to yearn for that connection. The more that researchers discover, the more we learn about how two people become attracted and how we can seek, find, and keep that love in ways that help both us and our beloveds to thrive.

In my work as a psychologist, I help people to understand how their life experiences, from early childhood up to the present day, can shape their expectations, their subconscious habits, and their relationships with others – and how, if those patterns are leading them away from the happiness they deserve, they can change them for the better. *Love: the Psychology of Attraction* will help you make a similar journey.

Every page is created to be as accessible as possible, with step-by-step advice, simple exercises, and scientific features revealing key studies and experiments. Rather than having to wade through dense psychology papers, you can read the findings of my colleagues in a style that's easy on the eyes and the brain: the science is both fascinating and encouraging for anyone who is searching for love.

This book takes you through the process of finding love. You'll begin with the most fundamental part of finding a relationship, and also the most often overlooked: your relationship with yourself. You, after all, are what you'll be bringing to the relationship, and the science suggests that those of us who can get our own psyches in good order are the most likely to have the happiest relationships. After this, the book then goes through the stages of searching for a partner: meeting new people, how to identify a great prospect and how to spot a waste of time, and how to steer a safe, sane course through the choppy waters of the dating scene.

You'll also learn about the psychology of establishing and maintaining a solid relationship in the long term. Having just picked up this book, it's likely that you're fairly early in this process, but do read the later chapters: if a solid long-term relationship is what you're aiming for, knowing what you want equips you to weed out those who don't want or can't offer it.

To be clear: love is your biological foundation – your ancestral legacy. It's love that makes us human, and it's love that keeps us alive as a species. Some of us are luckier in finding it than others, but if luck hasn't been running your way, a bit of knowledge might just be what you need to give it a push in the right direction. A book can't conjure up Mr. or Ms. Right, but what it can do is build your confidence, your psychological health, and your positive habits. It can help you to nurture a greater capacity to give and receive love, and send you into the dating scene as a newly informed expert. The world is full of people who want love, and one of them might just be right for you.

Leslie Becker-Phelps, Ph.D.

CHAPTER 1
YOU
ARE YOU READY FOR LOVE?

EVOLUTION CALLING
WHY WE FALL IN LOVE

Sometimes the longing for a partner can be so strong it seems irrational. If we look at what human beings are evolved to be, though, that longing makes perfect sense: we became what we are through love.

What kind of relationships did humans evolve for? Charles Darwin's theory of evolution talks of "survival of the fittest", but "fitness", in Darwin's terms, doesn't mean the strongest, the fastest, or the best. It means the best adapted to their particular environment. If there's nothing to eat but bamboo leaves, a speedy Kung Fu panda running around wasting energy is less likely to survive than the slow one that sits tight and makes those meals count. So what, in human terms, are we best adapted to, and why do we long for love?

> It is in our nature to nurture and be nurtured.
>
> **Bruce Perry**
> American psychiatrist

Born to connect
The first and foremost of all our human survival skills is sustaining relationships. Some animals are ready to run within minutes of being born. We humans are born helpless, and need care from a parent figure to survive our early years. But babies are demanding and exhausting, as any mother can tell you, and a mother needs motivation if she's going to do the work. The reward for all that toil is love. As John Bowlby, the British psychologist, psychoanalyst, and father of attachment theory (which we'll look at on page 16), put it in 1957: "Babies' smiles are powerful things leaving mothers spellbound and enslaved. Who can doubt that the baby who most readily rewards his mother with a smile is the one who is best loved and best cared for?"

EARLY ATTACHMENT

Developed by his student Mary Ainsworth, whose findings are shown in the chart below, John Bowlby's attachment theory became the foundation of what we now believe about how people relate to others and, in many ways, to themselves.

Attachment style	Parenting style	Child's baseline emotional state	Child's expectations of life
Secure	Warm, attentive, relatively consistent, and quick to respond	Happy, confident, and curious	"My needs will be met."
Anxious (*Ainsworth called this style "ambivalent/resistant"*)	Inconsistent: sometimes responsive and sometimes not	Insecure, anxious, and intensely emotional	"If I act in the right ways, I might earn love and my needs may be met."
Avoidant	Distant and cold, or harsh and critical	Emotionally shut-down	"I can't trust anyone to meet my needs. I must meet my own needs."

The love quiz

In 1985 the *Rocky Mountain News* in Denver, Colorado, asked its readers to choose one of three statements:

1 *I find it relatively easy to get close to others and am comfortable depending on them. I don't often worry about being abandoned or about someone getting too close to me.*

2 *I find that others are reluctant to get as close as I would like. I often worry that my partner doesn't really love me or won't want to stay with me. I want to get very close to my partner, and this sometimes scares people away.*

3 *I am somewhat uncomfortable being close to others; I find it difficult to trust them completely, difficult to allow myself to depend on them. I am nervous when anyone gets too close, and often, love partners want me to be more intimate than I feel comfortable being.*

This test was designed by American psychologists Cindy Hazan and Philip Shaver to see whether the childhood expectations identified in Bowlby and Ainsworth's attachment theory also carried over into adulthood. The results confirmed that those expectations do indeed persist.

Once you understand which of the attachment styles sounds most like yours – secure, anxious, or avoidant – then you are well on your way to understanding your romantic needs. To assess your attachment style, take a look at the chart overleaf.

In 1987, psychologists Cindy Hazan and Philip Shaver reported the results of their **love quiz:** **56 per cent** of adult respondents had identified themselves as **secure**, 19 per cent as **anxious**, and 25 per cent as **avoidant**.

56% SECURE

19% ANXIOUS

25% AVOIDANT

»

Which are you?

Estimates for how many of us display each attachment style have been revised over the course of many studies since the "love quiz" in 1987: various percentages are cited today, including the ones shown here, but it's impossible to get definitive figures. "Secure", "anxious", and "avoidant" aren't rigid boxes, more a sliding scale that encompasses many different personality types – two people with the same attachment style can be complete opposites in everything else! As broad groups, though, attachment styles are a useful way to look at love, since our styles – our needs – govern our relationships.

It's also worth noting that a minority of people can show both anxious and avoidant qualities – often because they've had very bad experiences in the past, especially in childhood. If that sounds like you, it can be helpful to learn about both styles. It's a painful combination, so you may also want to consider seeking out professional help from a supportive therapist.

The perfect combination

Secure people tend to have the most secure relationships, and a relationship needs only one secure partner to get that stability. With a partner happy to give reassurance and not threatened by the idea of being needed, an anxious person can relax, and is often loyal and loving. With someone who doesn't take it personally when their partner wants time alone, avoidant people can worry less about being tied down – most of the compromises in the relationship, though, will probably be made by the secure partner.

The real problem comes when two insecure types get together, as you'll see over the page. If relationships often get messy for you, learning to recognize attachment styles and understanding how they clash can give you a path through the conflict.

DISCOVER YOUR ATTACHMENT STYLE

Approximate percentage of the US population (3–5 per cent are "fearful avoidant")	When a relationship is under stress	What you are hypervigilant for
50% SECURE	I want to solve the problem. I can get upset, but I try to communicate clearly. If we're fighting, I try to stay on the subject rather than making it a fight about the whole relationship.	I'm not really the hypervigilant type, or at least not when it comes to relationship issues.
20% ANXIOUS	I get upset and do things I probably shouldn't, such as phoning all day, sulking, or making accusations. *(Psychologists call this "protest" behaviour: you really want to be reassured, but you don't often have the confidence to ask straight out.)*	Possible signs of rejection.
25% AVOIDANT	I tend to shut down emotionally in order to avoid dealing with it, but in my mind I run my partner down. *(This is known as "deactivating" your emotions: if you devalue your partner, losing them looks less scary.)*	Possible signs of being "tied down" in a relationship, or of having too much demanded of me.

To check which of the three main attachment styles below most resembles yours, read across each row and see if the scenarios it describes sound familiar.:

How you feel about emotional intimacy	How you view your partner's feelings	When apart from your partner	Who drives the relationship	Your reaction after a breakup
Of course I want to be close with my partner – that's how relationships work – but I also like to have space for following my own interests.	My responsibility is to support and nurture, just as he/she should feel responsible for my feelings. We're a team here.	I may miss him/her, but I know the relationship is safe and I can concentrate fine on other matters.	It's not really an issue: we each get our way some of the time, and try to work things out to our mutual satisfaction.	I grieve for a while, then seek a new relationship. After all, I deserve to be loved.
I really want to be close, but showing my neediness will probably drive people away.	Most of all, I want them to feel love for me. I'm fearful that they'll lose interest in me as soon as my performance falters. I can be very supportive if feeling confident, but I still need regular reassurance that they love me or else I'll worry that they don't.	I worry that they'll forget me or find someone else; I can get very distracted if the worry escalates, although often small, timely gestures such as a quick text message can get me back on track.	How a relationship goes is mostly down to my partner. If I lose them, I feel I'll never find someone else who wants me.	I cling to the remnants of a finished relationship after I should have got over it. I tend to blame myself and can need a long time to recover.
I don't want to be hassled – I need my space. *(In fact, avoidants do still need love, like everyone else, but their mistrust means a strong need for feelings of independence.)*	My partner's feelings are their problem. Everyone should be able to stand on their own two feet, and it's off-putting if they try to load their neediness onto me. I don't like a lot of drama.	I often experience feelings for my partner most deeply when we're apart. But when we're together again, their faults can irritate me, and my fear of intimacy and of being let down returns.	Try to control me and I'm gone. *(An avoidant type often sees control as an either/or – either one person has the control or the other does – and may use confusion or mixed signals to keep the upper hand.)*	I put it out of my mind and move on as fast as possible. *(Sometimes, though, avoidants idealize a lost ex – not because the ex was perfect, but because it helps deactivate feelings for a new partner.)*

CLASHING EXPECTATIONS
WHEN INSECURE TYPES GET TOGETHER

It's generally acknowledged that relationships do best when at least one partner has a secure attachment style. But what if neither does? Understanding the challenge of insecure styles – anxious or avoidant – can help you to avoid certain pitfalls.

When two anxious people fall in love

The relationship may be close, even passionate, but there's likely to be a lot of conflict when both partners "protest" (see page 18) instead of communicating their feelings directly. Fights can escalate with neither partner understanding why. If the relationship lasts, it'll always be volatile; if it ends, it's likely to end in mutual recrimination and confusion.

When two avoidants fall in love

This pairing isn't very common in long-term relationships: with neither party seeking to grow close, the couple can just drift apart. If they do stay together, it can become more a marriage of convenience than a true partnership – possibly with mutual infidelities and decreasing respect for the other, and probably with both partners getting most of their

❤ WHEN NICE GIRLS FALL FOR BAD BOYS

Remember Bridget Jones and her diary? One reason for the story's huge success is that it is a pitch-perfect portrait of the three attachment styles and how they bounce off each other. A lot of chick lit stories can be read as "Nice girl falls for bad boy then finds good man", but a more psychological way of putting it would be "Anxious person falls for avoidant person, then finds happiness with secure person". (If you've read the book or seen the movie, you'll know Bridget panics over nothing and does silly things as a result: that's hypervigilance and protest in action.) For all the anxious people out there, finding a secure partner is probably the happy ending you're looking for.

emotional satisfaction elsewhere. Avoidant people need connection, even if they aren't comfortable with the idea, and another avoidant probably won't provide it.

The anxious-avoidant trap

This is probably the most disastrous combination of all, yet one of the most common. A person who feels unworthy and weaker and a person who needs to feel independent and stronger can reinforce each other's self-images and get stuck in an endless cycle of highs and lows. It's the anxious person who generally comes off worse, as it's far easier to withhold intimacy than it is to compel it, and these relationships can damage an anxious person's self-esteem for years (see pages 148–149).

In either case, your best bet is generally to look for a person who is secure, or at the secure end of the spectrum if they are anxious or avoidant. If you are secure yourself, you may be able to find love with an anxious or avoidant person – though if you want intimacy, anxious is probably a better bet than avoidant – but if you're insecure, remember that your needs are your needs whatever they are, and you have a right to a partner who takes them seriously.

Gender stereotypes?

A lot of self-help advice in popular culture assumes that "anxious" is the natural style for women and that "avoidant" is the natural style for men. If you've read John Gray's *Men Are From Mars, Women Are From Venus*, you may remember his rubber-band simile, arguing that men need to draw away to feel themselves pulled back to their partners – a vivid

IT'S ALL IN HOW YOU LOOK AT IT

When clashing attachment styles get together, it can be hard for them to see each other's needs as legitimate: when your needs are so different from your partner's, sometimes it feels as if one of you must be crazy, and probably you'd rather it was them. A secure partner will likely perceive your needs more positively, and may use different words to describe them. Which would you rather someone called you?

ANXIOUS

An avoidant partner calls it...	A secure partner calls it...
■ Clingy	✔ Affectionate
■ Needy	✔ Worried
■ Melodramatic	✔ Upset
■ Demanding	✔ Companionable
■ Commitment-obsessed	✔ Loyal

AVOIDANT

An anxious partner calls it...	A secure partner calls it...
■ Distant	✔ Private
■ Confusing	✔ Cautious
■ Selfish	✔ Self-sufficient
■ Mean	✔ Conflicted
■ Commitment-phobic	✔ Independent

description of how avoidant people work. In reality, though, there are plenty of anxious men and avoidant women out there.

If you don't understand how the attachment system works, it's easy to think you're being either "clingy" or "selfish". Describing yourself as a "typical" woman or man helps allay the embarrassment: if it's typical for your gender, it's not your fault, right?

Actually, the explanation is more likely to lie in your attachment system than your gender. With a more secure partner, both anxious and avoidant people can have fulfilling relationships, no matter what sex they are. The important thing to remember is this: neither sex has a monopoly on difficult childhoods or bad experiences, and whatever your sex, secure people outnumber avoidants two to one.

GREAT EXPECTATIONS

MENTAL IMAGES OF OURSELVES AND OTHER PEOPLE

Early in life we start to form our ideas about what people are like, including ourselves. Those mental templates shape our romantic expectations – and, consequently, our romantic experiences.

Society is a big place and we need some kind of mental map to navigate it, which is why we are evolved to absorb and learn from birth. From observing our parents and others around us, we start to draw conclusions about what we can expect of people. In effect, we make two mental models, one labelled "What am I like?" and the other "What are other people like?" Social psychologists Kim Bartholomew and Leonard Horowitz related these models to attachment theory in the 1990s, in a four-category model of attachment (see opposite).

When your needs are met

A person who grows up in a nurturing environment is going to have some positive models of themselves and of others. When your needs are generally met, you start to feel you must be a worthwhile person because that's how you're being treated. Meanwhile, other people are reliable and kind, and your inner picture of humanity has a

> ...early attachment relations come to form a prototype for later relationships outside the family.
>
> **Kim Bartholomew and Leonard M. Horowitz**
> in the *Journal of Personality and Social Psychology*

positive glow to it; when you have a negative experience, you find ways to smooth over it. You carry that glow through childhood and into your relationships as an adult.

When your needs aren't met

If the people responsible for you don't meet your emotional needs well enough, you're going to develop a negative perception of yourself. You sense "there must be something

wrong with me". You then feel you must overcome your personal faults to earn the love and acceptance of others. The conclusion you draw is that other people are more important and more powerful than you. Your model of "self" is negative, but your model of "other" is positive. That makes for anxiety in relationships: if you feel inferior to other people, it's hard to feel you deserve their love.

A person who feels attacked or whose needs aren't acknowledged, let alone met, loses their trust in people: "I've got to take care of myself, I can't rely on anyone else." Once you've sealed yourself off from disappointment, who needs other people? Feeling you can trust yourself, your model of "self" is positive, but your model of "other" is negative. Emotional intimacy is risky, and to be avoided, because it means shackling your trustworthy self to an untrustworthy other.

Really bad experiences can make us write off ourselves and others. If you suffered serious abuse in your childhood, for example, it's not unusual to grow up feeling bad about

What am I like?

YOUR MENTAL MAP

In this model of attachment – which includes "fearful" as a fourth style – our expectations of ourselves and other people can create different attachment styles that shape how we relate to our partners.

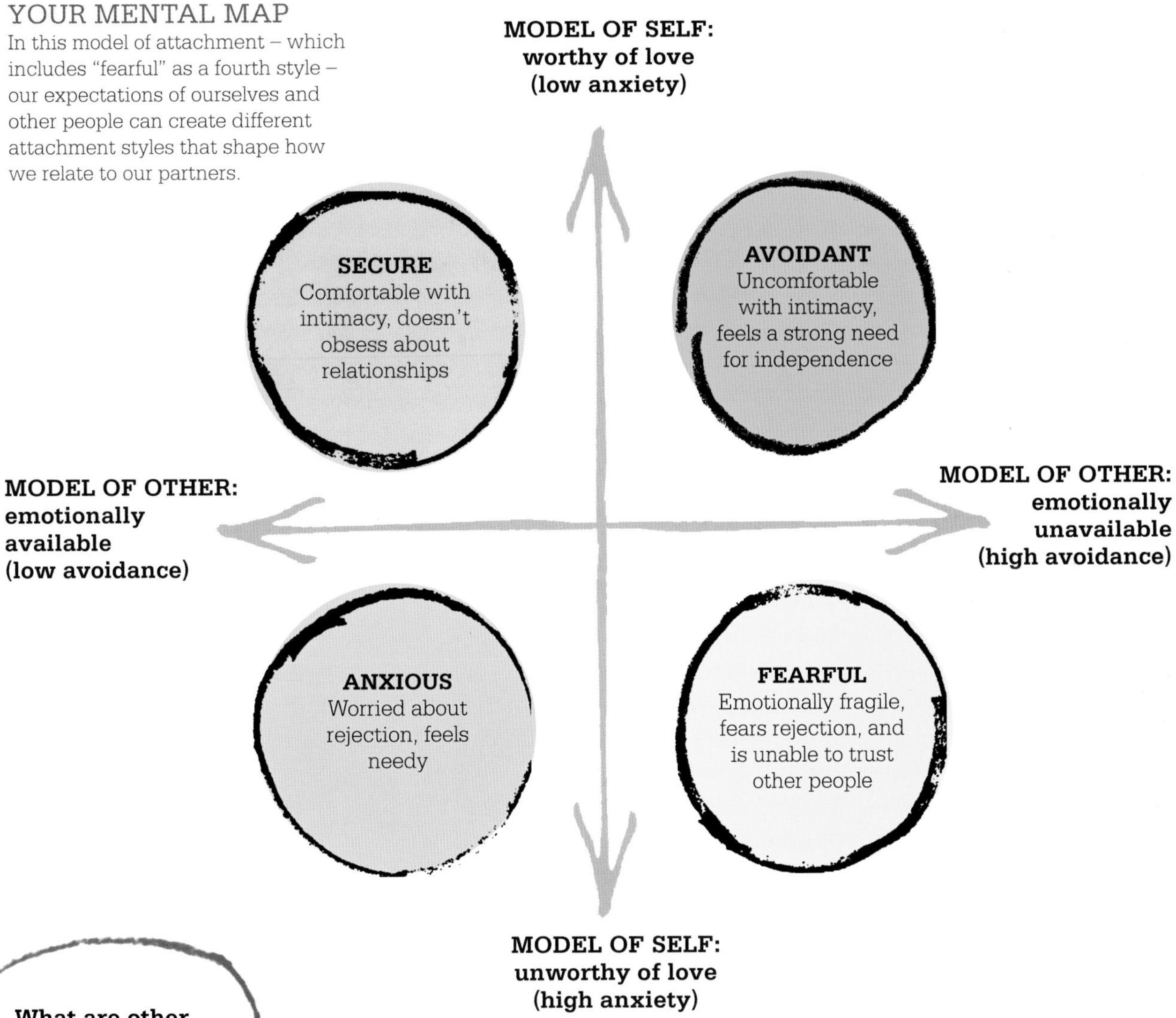

MODEL OF SELF:
worthy of love
(low anxiety)

SECURE
Comfortable with intimacy, doesn't obsess about relationships

AVOIDANT
Uncomfortable with intimacy, feels a strong need for independence

MODEL OF OTHER:
emotionally
available
(low avoidance)

MODEL OF OTHER:
emotionally
unavailable
(high avoidance)

ANXIOUS
Worried about rejection, feels needy

FEARFUL
Emotionally fragile, fears rejection, and is unable to trust other people

MODEL OF SELF:
unworthy of love
(high anxiety)

What are other people like?

yourself and scared to trust anyone else. Many abuse survivors go on to have happy and fulfilling relationships, so a hard start in life doesn't necessarily lead to singledom: your first step is probably to seek out a trustworthy therapist who can help you work on healing your wounds. You should always pursue therapy for your own sake – do it because you

deserve to feel good about yourself – and you may also find that addressing past trauma can make you far better able to create future happiness.

Feeling better
With work and patience, we can adjust our models for a kinder view of life. Some of us start out doubting we're worthy of being loved; some of us doubt whether other people can be trusted not to hurt us if we do give

them our hearts. Self-affirmation (see pages 34–35) and self-compassion (on pages 54–57) can help you tackle those fears, as can CBT, or Cognitive Behavioural Therapy (coming up next). The starting point, of course, is to know just what we're afraid of: when we are able to understand our expectations, a lot of problems look less overwhelming – including the tricky business of finding and creating love.

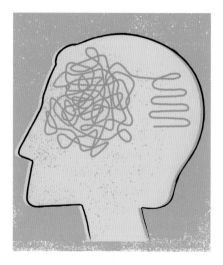

THINKING STRAIGHT

HOW NOT TO TALK YOURSELF DOWN

Do you ever find you're thinking yourself into a pit of despair? Cognitive Behavioural Therapy (CBT) is a straightforward way to identify how you tend to get into that pit – and then think yourself back out again.

THE NEGATIVITY TRAP

Thoughts, feelings, and behaviour are all intertwined, and can end up sending you round in a circle, as shown below. Following the CBT model, you can break the cycle by first addressing the negative thought.

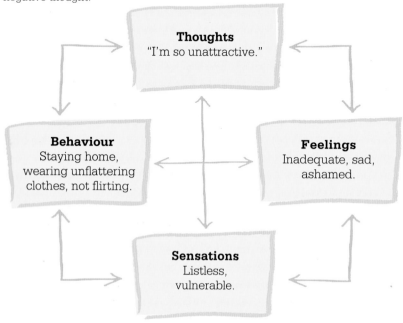

Thoughts
"I'm so unattractive."

Feelings
Inadequate, sad, ashamed.

Sensations
Listless, vulnerable.

Behaviour
Staying home, wearing unflattering clothes, not flirting.

Cognitive Behavioural Therapy is a popular form of treatment for anxiety that proposes that our thought patterns keep us trapped in cycles of stress and worry. The theory runs thus: we begin with a negative thought. The negative thought causes painful feelings, which in turn affect how we act and think. The solution, by this logic, is to tackle the problem at source and challenge the upsetting thoughts before they make us feel worse.

The way to challenge the negativity trap is to try to find any "cognitive distortions" in it. CBT identifies ten, listed oppposite. If you find yourself thinking your way into the blues, try the following exercise:

- What's the thought or the belief that's bothering me?
- How strongly – what percentage – do I believe that it's true?
- Are there any cognitive distortions going on here?
- Could there be another, more positive, interpretation of events?
- What's the percentage now?

Remember, you don't need to get the percentage down to zero; reducing it by a bit can build up, over time, to a happier way of thinking.

ARE YOU PRONE TO ANY OF THESE COGNITIVE DISTORTIONS?

Distortion	Description	Example
All-or-nothing thinking	Thinking in black and white terms: if you're not perfect, you're a total loser.	"Nobody's going to find me attractive with this huge nose of mine."
Overgeneralizing	Drawing wider conclusions from limited or insufficient information.	"He forgot to call me – I knew he didn't care about me."
Mental filter	Screening out the good things so that only the bad stick in your mind.	"She made dinner while I did my taxes, but if she loved me she'd have helped with the form."
Disqualifying the positive	Explaining away your own good points or positive experiences.	"He said I have lovely eyes, but people only praise your eyes when your face is plain."
Jumping to conclusions	"Mind reading" (eg, assuming that others are thinking ill of you) and "fortune telling" (eg, predicting disaster as if it were a certainty).	"I was late for our date – she must think I'm an idiot who can't catch a train. She's going to dump me, I know it."
Magnification (or catastrophizing) and minimization	Blowing bad things out of proportion and predicting disaster and/or underrating the importance of good things.	"I can't believe he forgot that book I asked to borrow. He's never going to keep his promises to me!"
Emotional reasoning	Drawing a conclusion that things are bad because you feel bad.	"I feel so unattractive. Nobody will ever want me."
"Should" statements	Beating up on yourself – and others – with unnecessarily prescriptive demands.	"If this relationship was working, we should be planning a holiday together by now."
Labelling and mislabelling	Applying highly loaded labels to yourself and others.	"It's been so long since I had a date – I'm just undateable."
Personalization	Thinking that a negative event must have been caused by you somehow.	"He's put off our date until tomorrow – I must look too needy."

LET'S FALL IN LOVE

HOW SUSCEPTIBLE ARE YOU?

Why do some of us fall in love quickly and some of us never quite feel we have fallen in love? The answer may lie in our past attachments: our own attitudes can be as important as meeting the right person.

 WHICH OF THESE SOUNDS LIKE YOU?

When I meet someone attractive, I first think about:
A Whether they'll be interested in me, and reasons they might not be.
B Whether they're up for some fun.
C Whether we'll get along with each other.

On a date, I watch for:
A Signs that I might be putting my date off.
B Signs that my date wants to get too serious.
C Signs that my date will treat me nicely.

In a relationship, I usually:
A Feel like the one who loves more.
B Feel under pressure to commit.
C Feel like we're in a partnership.

If we hit a rough patch, I will:
A Worry that no one else will want me if this ends.

B Decide to cut it short – why bother?
C Try to make it work – but if the relationship has to end, so be it.

If I'm single for a while, I:
A Worry that I'll be alone for ever, and might date someone just to reassure myself.
B Enjoy the freedom, and enjoy having fun.
C Try to enjoy life – it's better to wait than be with the wrong person.

Mostly A: You have elements of anxious attachment style.
Mostly B: You have elements of avoidant attachment style.
Mostly C: You have elements of secure attachment style.

Most of us are a mixture, but our fears may be caused by our predominant attachment style – not by our being undesirable or others being unworthy!

We all know people who never stay single for long and who feel each new relationship is true love at last. We all know people, too, who date partner after partner, many of whom seem lovely but never quite capture their heart. Maybe we're even that person ourselves. Why do some people fall in love so easily while others don't?

What's going on?
While it may be that some people have a knack of flirting and attract a wider choice of partners, even the most sought-after person dating the most charming suitor doesn't necessarily fall in love right away. The explanation may lie in our image of ourselves and others.

If we're anxious, we tend to feel inadequate and hungry for love, which can make us hasty. If we assume everyone is too good for us, we're less likely to look at a partner critically before giving them our hearts. Anxious people fall in love quickly – not always wrong if their partner is a great person, but if there's an incompatibility, heartache may follow. If you're anxious, you need to be sure you have emotional intimacy and trust as well as passion, to avoid mistaking excitement for love.

STERNBERG'S TRIANGULAR THEORY OF LOVE

American psychologist Robert Sternberg suggests that love is made up of three components: passion, closeness (which he calls intimacy), and commitment. If you are avoidant, you may be trying to steer clear of commitment as well as intimacy, but if you're anxious, you may jump to commit before you're truly intimate. Where on the triangle do you usually fall, and what kind of love are you looking for?

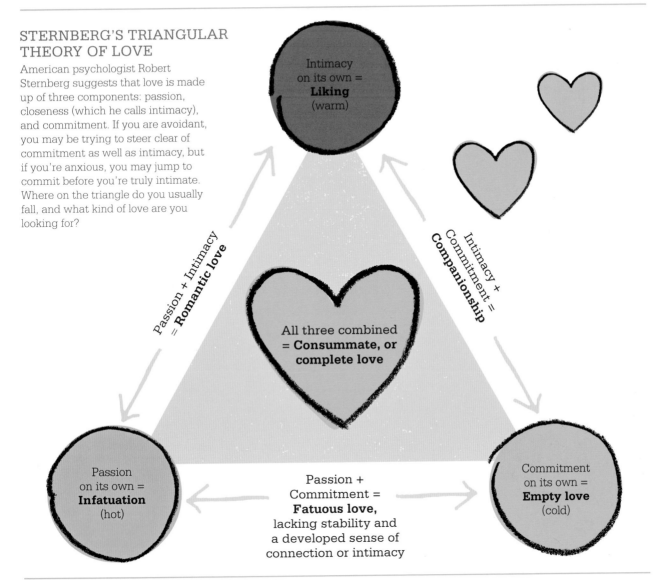

Intimacy on its own = **Liking** (warm)

Passion + Intimacy = **Romantic love**

Intimacy + Commitment = **Companionship**

All three combined = **Consummate, or complete love**

Passion on its own = **Infatuation** (hot)

Passion + Commitment = **Fatuous love,** lacking stability and a developed sense of connection or intimacy

Commitment on its own = **Empty love** (cold)

Dreaming of perfection

If we're avoidant, deep down we're scared of getting hurt and so we make a habit of keeping our feelings on lockdown for safety's sake. Avoidant people may not consider themselves unromantic: on the contrary, many avoidants dream of "the one", the perfect ideal they're holding out for. It's not unusual, either, for avoidants to remain in love with an ex-partner, longing for a lost love. Both of these can be deactivating strategies: if only the perfect "one" will do, it's easier to stay invulnerable around an imperfect partner – that is, any real person who might get close to you and possibly hurt you. The lost love can have the same effect: probably during the relationship you were keenly aware of their faults – they weren't the perfect "one" either, since no one is perfect – and you can only focus on their good points now they're gone. Avoidants may really want love, but also want to avoid dealing with a real person's flaws and needs, and stick to the safety of fantasy instead. Real love can take time, and flourishes best in a secure relationship.

The best way to help yourself is to try to be clear about which feelings are being caused by other people and which are caused by your own anxieties – no easy task, but well worth it. To get that clarity, start by taking the quiz opposite; do any of these habits sound familiar?

WHY DO I NEVER LEARN?

THE SECRET OF REPEATING PATTERNS

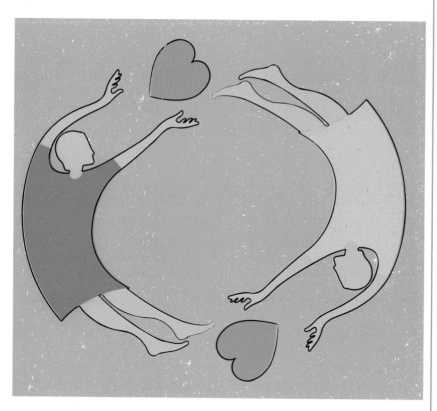

Do you keep swearing you'll never make the same mistake, only to find that the next relationship has the same problems as the last one? Then it's worth examining your needs and your choices.

In the 1980s, American therapist Harville Hendrix proposed the Imago theory: we are driven by the need to develop ourselves as human beings, and our subconscious images about our primary caregivers in childhood steer us towards partners who could help us develop. The early experiences we have in life may be supportive or neglectful, forgiving or punitive; no one is perfect, not even our caregivers, and by the time we reach the age of romance, most of us are carrying a few unresolved issues.

How many people do you know who keep getting involved with the same kind of unsuitable person – the woman who is attracted to men like her father, even if he was a bully, or the man who can't seem to take an interest in anyone who's interested in him? Might you be one of those people yourself? We all want to be happy, so choosing people who make us unhappy seems odd. Imago theory argues that our repeating patterns are an attempt to be happy – but in a slightly unexpected way.

Healing old wounds

No one gets to adulthood without taking some knocks along the way, and deep down we want to heal those bruises. Imago therapist Bruce Crapuchettes suggests, "We are

> We're born into relationship, and it's in relationship that we find healing and growth and potential.
>
> **Bruce Crapuchettes**
> Imago therapist

drawn to someone who's going to trigger our unfinished business … because of this urge inside to grow and maximize potential." So we unconsciously choose partners who remind us of past experiences and who therefore – we hope – offer us the chance to heal old wounds.

The problem comes if we try to resolve unfinished business by changing our partner rather than by understanding the issues they trigger and asking for their support. If, for example, you fear abandonment, you may feel anxious when your partner goes out with their friends. You can't keep them home every night, but if you say clearly that you feel insecure and want to be reassured they look forward to coming back to you, that can help both of you.

Finding new safety

If you keep making the same mistakes, what do they have in common? In past relationships that have gone wrong, what wound might you have been trying to heal? While searching for love, remember that a romantic relationship isn't the only way to heal ourselves: we can also work on feeling better about ourselves (see pages 54–57). By separating the wish for a partner and the need to heal, you can feel less hurried as you seek new partners.

Addressing old insecurities has to be mutual, so we need a partner who is willing to work with us. If you find someone who'll collaborate on mutual healing, you may find that old mistakes turn into new confidence. Never forget that if you present your needs constructively, you have the right to a partner who supports them. If you find yourself trying to fix a partner rather than communicate with them, try the three keys shown on the right, and see if these make the conversation go any better.

 ## THREE KEYS TO EFFECTIVE COMMUNICATION

For you or your partner to help the other to heal old wounds, there are three keys to a constructive discussion of needs:

1 Mirroring
Repeat back what your partner says to be sure you've understood, and make it clear to them that you're taking what they say on board.

> It annoys me when you don't call – it makes me feel like you've forgotten I exist.

> So, when I don't call, you get annoyed that I've forgotten you?

2 Validation
Acknowledge their right to their feelings. You don't have to agree with their opinion – they may be worried about something illogical – but their feelings are real to them. Show you accept that.

> Stop leaving the milk out, it drives me crazy! I feel like I'm surrounded by chaos.

> I can see how having things lying around feels chaotic. I don't want to make you feel that way.

3 Empathy
Try to see it from their point of view. Again, you don't have to agree with that viewpoint, but make it clear that you know their feelings are as valid as yours.

> When I saw you talking to your ex, I felt really insecure, and I couldn't say anything without disrupting the party.

> I can understand that must have been uncomfortable for you, especially if you didn't feel free to talk about it.

GIVING UP YOUR INDEPENDENCE?
HOW TO BALANCE AUTONOMY AND CONNECTION

Many of us fear that taking on a relationship means giving up our freedom and identity. In reality, a healthy relationship can be a support while also giving us greater independence. It's all about interdependence.

If a toddler takes a painful tumble, he may cry – and then he'll run to his mum for a cuddle. His mum, if she's attentive, will pick him up, give him kisses and kind words, and quite quickly he'll feel better, climb off her lap, and run back to his play.

The toddler is using his bond with his mother for "affect regulation" – keeping his emotions at a fairly manageable level. His mother is his "secure base", supporting him and encouraging him to head out into the world. She is also his "safe haven", the place he can go back to when things get too much, a resting point of love where he can recover. That's a need we don't grow out of.

Managing our feelings

Even the most secure of us can have a difficult day. Our boss scolds us, or our granny is sick – all these knocks can make us feel vulnerable. What do we do when we're feeling that way?

Mostly, we turn to a safe haven for comfort. For adults, that's usually our romantic partner. Even if we can't

---

🔍 SURVIVAL SKILLS

In 2003, researcher Michael Meaney took a selection of rats and dropped them in a canister of water to sink or swim. Why? Meaney had closely observed the kind of mothers these rats had had as pups. Some rat mums licked and groomed their pups a lot; some were less nurturing. The best-loved pups, when dropped in water, kept their heads and swam, while the less-licked went to pieces and, had they not been fished out again, would have probably drowned. Having a safe haven can make us independent in a crisis – literally to the point of life or death.

run straight into their arms, a secure couple can feel calmed just by thinking of each other, knowing the partner is in their life and available to comfort them later on. A secure base empowers us to strike out alone and run back to our play.

When we're insecure

Not all of us can direct our feelings so easily. While it's healthy to look to our partner to help us regulate our feelings, the anxious person *needs* their partner to do this and can get upset with the partner if they don't. A secure partner may be willing to provide this if they can, but it's healthier if we learn to calm ourselves: no one can be there all the time, and we need to be able to cope with that (see the exercises on pages 56–57). Anxious attachment doesn't vanish overnight, and all of us want support in managing our feelings sometimes – but the better we are

at calming ourselves, the better we'll be able to ask for support calmly and constructively when our partner does get free to talk.

An avoidant person, on the other hand, tends to dismiss both their own feelings and offers of help – driven by the fear that others can't be trusted to be there for them, and by the compensating belief that a strong, competent person shouldn't need help. While secure and anxious people are usually reassured by offers of support, avoidant people can find them threatening. Accepting the offer feels like giving up some of our self-reliance and acknowledging that we might need other people after all – which plays right into our fear that they'll let us down.

If you're used to handling painful feelings by disconnecting from them, others may end up feeling rejected and undervalued when you turn down their offers of support. Yet interdependence is not the same

thing as dependence. A partner who controls you is a bad choice, but a partner who counts on you and who you can count on can make it easier for you to manage out in the world.

POURING YOUR HEART OUT

A study published in 2000 in the *Journal of Personal and Social Psychology* recorded 93 people disclosing a personal problem to their boyfriend or girlfriend. While the more avoidant partners fell short on giving support, and the more anxious partners weren't good at asking for it, the people who could relate securely reported that the care of their partner made them feel better. Being able to trust a partner to help us pick ourselves up makes it easier to face life's challenges.

KEEP IN TOUCH AND KEEP ON TRACK

If you are anxious, you may feel the need for reassurance at points when your partner doesn't have much time to give it. The good news is that anxious people are usually easy to reassure – a quick SMS is often all it takes.

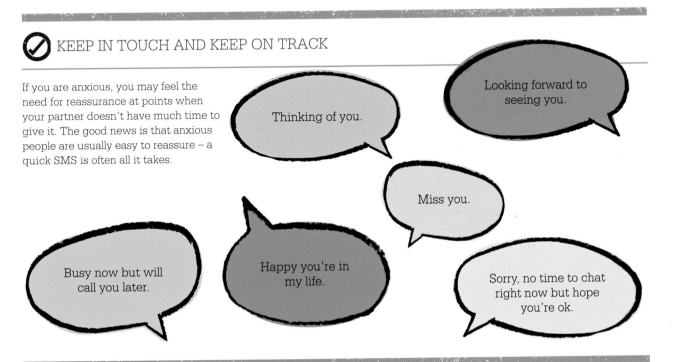

Thinking of you.

Looking forward to seeing you.

Miss you.

Busy now but will call you later.

Happy you're in my life.

Sorry, no time to chat right now but hope you're ok.

YOUR OWN WORST ENEMY?

HOW MENTAL HABITS HINDER OR HELP

We all want to be happy, so why do some of us stay in situations that make us miserable? Perhaps because we also want to avoid confusion. If we expect problems, trouble can be perversely reassuring.

CHALLENGING YOUR EXPECTATIONS

Take on this daily exercise: start noting your selective thinking and find ways to create more positive habits.

Challenge selective attention:
- What nice things did people do for you today?
- How did you feel about it?
- Did you dismiss it? If so, how?

Challenge selective memory:
- What good stuff did you do today?
- How did people react?
- Did it show they cared about you?

Challenge selective interpretation:
- Think about an incident today that made you feel bad.
- Is there a more positive spin you could put on it?
- Are you over-generalizing?
- Are you stressing people's bad points or downplaying their good?

Would you say you're an optimist? Do you expect life to go well and people to like you? If someone says nice things about you, do you feel reassured or disconcerted?

No one really wants to be treated badly. But along with the desire for connection and love goes another basic human need: to have a clear sense of who we are. Having our identity called into question is deeply disturbing, and most of us will go to some lengths to avoid it.

So what is your identity?

If you see yourself as a lovable person living in a world where people are pretty decent, a warm and devoted partner will confirm that, and a mean or disinterested partner will jar. Staying with the nice one and leaving the other makes sense, right?

But suppose you feel yourself to be basically unlovable. A partner who loves you may be what you need, but on some level it's confusing: they're treating you like someone you're not (at least in your own mind). A partner who doesn't love you is painful, but at least it makes sense to you – they aren't forcing you to question your sense of yourself – and we generally accept what makes sense.

Unconsciously, we can push for what we expect. American psychologist William Swann dubbed this phenomenon "self-verification", and it can make us act against our own interests. In 1988, Swann tested college students by seeing whether they preferred roommates who rated them favourably or negatively: the students who liked themselves avoided the negative roommates, but the students with poor self-image

> Self-verification processes are driven by people's desire to maximize their perceptions of predictability and control.
>
> **William Swann**
> American psychologist

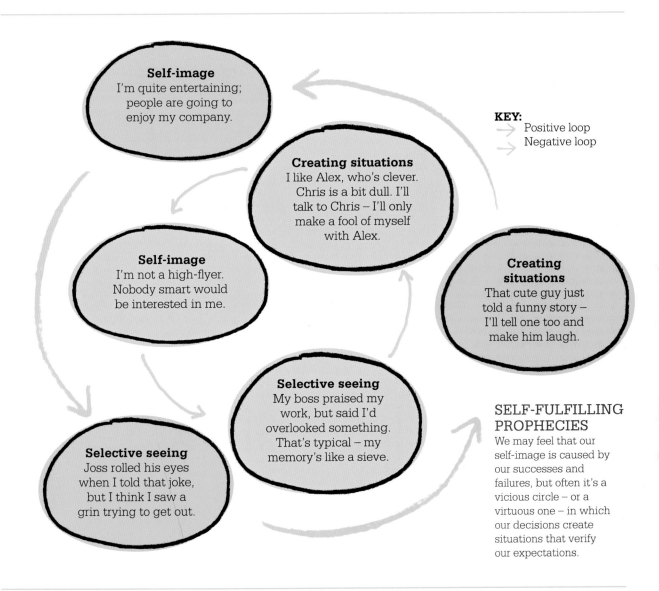

Self-image
I'm quite entertaining; people are going to enjoy my company.

KEY:
→ Positive loop
→ Negative loop

Creating situations
I like Alex, who's clever. Chris is a bit dull. I'll talk to Chris – I'll only make a fool of myself with Alex.

Self-image
I'm not a high-flyer. Nobody smart would be interested in me.

Creating situations
That cute guy just told a funny story – I'll tell one too and make him laugh.

Selective seeing
My boss praised my work, but said I'd overlooked something. That's typical – my memory's like a sieve.

Selective seeing
Joss rolled his eyes when I told that joke, but I think I saw a grin trying to get out.

SELF-FULFILLING PROPHECIES

We may feel that our self-image is caused by our successes and failures, but often it's a vicious circle – or a virtuous one – in which our decisions create situations that verify our expectations.

actually preferred the roommates who said bad things about them. The negative comments weren't pleasant, but did provide self-verification – and that's what informed their choice.

Paying attention

In the same way, we tend to be selective in our attention, memory, and interpretation: if something confirms our self-image, we simply take it on board better. Even when

our partner is treating us well, if we still expect the worst – which anxious and avoidant types often do – we may be more aware of any bad moments than good ones, because the bad ones confirm our expectations. By focusing on the bad and overlooking the good, we might not realize how great someone is – or how great we are.

If you find your past relationships all left a bad taste, take some time to

consider this key question: do you feel lovable? And if not, that's an important place to start. You certainly do deserve nice treatment from people; everyone does. You just need to be your own best ally in seeking it out. Try some self-affirmation exercises (on the next page) and see if you can become open to changing your self-image.

YOU DESERVE THE BEST

HEALTHY POSITIVE THINKING

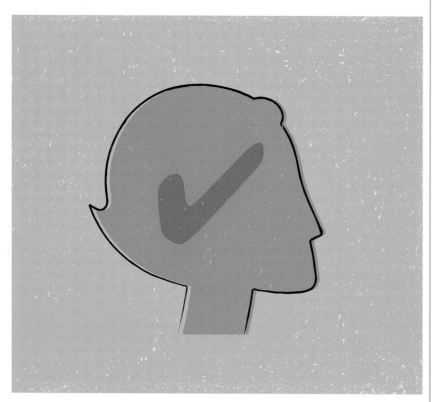

Evidence-based psychology – and our own experience – tells us that people who feel good about themselves are happier in relationships. To get started on that path to greater confidence, try some self-affirmation.

Do we need to be perfect to feel good about ourselves? The answer is a resounding "No": even the most confident people know there are things they can't do or qualities they lack. What we need, instead, is to have a sense of ourselves as generally worthwhile – that even if we have our faults, we also have good qualities that counterbalance them, adding up to a sense of overall value and integrity.

Accentuate the positive

We tend to spend a lot of time reflecting on how to fix ourselves. There are strategic advantages to that – sometimes problems need to be addressed – but if we dwell only on our problems and pitfalls, we're spending all our self-reflection time telling ourselves that things are wrong. That doesn't help us feel very lovable.

Self-affirmation theory emphasizes the importance of remembering our good points. Suppose, for instance, you have a terrible singing voice and feel embarrassed on karaoke night. If you think only about your singing, you're liable to end up feeling that you are ridiculous and unattractive, and that nobody could really be interested in you. If, on the other hand, you remind yourself of your best points, you put the negatives in context and give your self-esteem a

> You can reprogram your brain, which can affect how you feel and function.
>
> **Roya R. Rad**
> Psychologist, writing on self-affirmation in the *Huffington Post*

SELF-AFFIRMATION IN PRACTICE

Do you find you keep beating up on yourself? Make a habit of running through these steps and see if it makes you feel better.

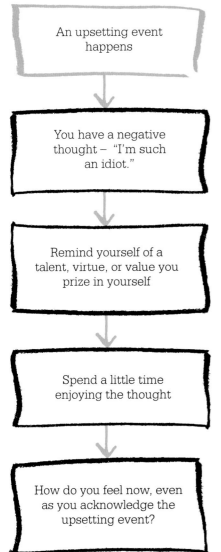

An upsetting event happens

↓

You have a negative thought – "I'm such an idiot."

↓

Remind yourself of a talent, virtue, or value you prize in yourself

↓

Spend a little time enjoying the thought

↓

How do you feel now, even as you acknowledge the upsetting event?

boost that offsets the singing. These qualities don't have to be relevant to karaoke – maybe you're a great cook, or a talented organizer. Whatever it is, in effect you can say, "Well, I can't sing, but never mind, I'm good at

other things." A well-meaning friend may tell you not to worry, your singing is, er, great – but if you know that's not true, false affirmation will probably make you feel worse. For self-affirmation to work, forget your wobbly singing and focus on those good points instead.

Creating resilience

Self-affirmation can have surprisingly wide-ranging effects. A study in 2009, for example, found that people who had done poorly on a maths test would usually be discouraged and perform equally badly a second time. Between the two tests, however, some were given a word search task that subtly reminded them of values that they'd previously stated were important to them – for instance, finding the word "colour" in the scrambled letters if they'd said they cared about art. Reminded of what they loved, they got over their first failure and performed the second maths test much better. In other words, just thinking of something they felt good about enabled people to show more skill at a less comfortable task.

Thinking of others

While self-affirmation can help us become more resilient and feel better about ourselves, positive psychology tells us that how we relate to the world around us is equally important. Greater wealth, for example, doesn't actually improve our happiness all that much once we have enough to cover our basic needs – but spending money on other people does. Three big predictors of happiness have been found to be optimism, gratitude, and altruism: by doing nice things for other people and dwelling on the nice things they've done for us, we may find we're feeling better about

ourselves without really trying. It's a pretty good bet that our loved ones will feel better towards us as well, creating a virtuous circle in which we can end up mutually appreciating each other. While you're in the process of affirming your own sense of value, positive psychology suggests you needn't stop at trying to find good things to say about yourself: when you do good things for other people, the satisfaction and pride will happen by themselves. Self-affirmation is about reminding ourselves of our positive qualities, which in turn may help us interact well in the world. We all feel out of our depth sometimes, but by giving mental space to the things you do well, you may find yourself doing better in unexpected ways – including feeling more lovable and more confident in the complicated world of romance.

TRY THESE THREE GOOD THINGS

Pioneered by US psychologist Martin Seligman, known as the father of positive psychology, this is an exercise to do every night before you go to sleep.

1 **Think of three good things that happened today.** These things don't need to be major; they could be as simple as "I had a nice lunch." Just as long as you enjoyed them.

2 **Write them down.**

3 **Reflect on why they happened.** You can find your own explanations, be it "The world is a beautiful place" or "I planned my day very smartly." The point is to let your brain experience the pleasure of following positive cause and effect.

EXTROVERT OR INTROVERT?

WHERE YOU DRAW YOUR ENERGY FROM

Some of us are reflective and quiet, while others are outgoing party animals. There's no right way to be, but knowing your own needs can help a lot, whether you are already dating or looking to move on.

Most of us are familiar with the terms "introvert" and "extrovert", but are they really personality descriptions? Each conjures up certain stereotypes: introvert is often taken to mean either brooding and neurotic or sensitive and intellectual, while extrovert can either be used to mean shallow and noisy or friendly and well-adjusted.

Beyond the stereotypes

In reality, there are plenty of popular, easy-going introverts and smart, sensitive extroverts. (There are also misanthropic extroverts and empty-headed introverts, but you probably don't want to date them.) First made popular by Swiss psychiatrist Carl Jung, and now widely used by employers in the Myers-Briggs psychometric tests, the two terms describe where you get your energy from. If being in company with other people makes you feel energized, while being alone wears you down, you're an extrovert. If you feel tired after interacting with people or being in a very stimulating environment, and you find it restful to do solitary activities, you're an introvert. Or you may be a mix of the two – an "ambivert". It's a sliding scale, and where you sit may equally depend on who's placing you on it: to a very introverted person, almost everyone looks extroverted, and vice versa. When Isabel Briggs Myers first estimated the ratios in the 1960s, she put America at about 25 per cent introvert and 75 per cent extrovert. In 1998, the Myers & Briggs Foundation's first official study revised the estimate to a pretty even split of 50.7 per cent introvert and 49.3 per cent extrovert.

Energy in love

How does this relate to finding love? Some people argue the best pairing is introvert-extrovert, as each balances the other out. Others say it's best to be with someone like yourself, as you'll enjoy the same things. It can be more useful to ask yourself what sort of environments favour you. If you're an introvert, you're unlikely to find your true love in a noisy club, as you won't be at your best there. If you are an extrovert, you may like a quiet walk in the park, but if you look for

> My introverted husband once told me, "Being with you is like being alone." It was his way of saying he loves my company: he meant that he never wants a break from me.

> My husband is extroverted. I'm introverted. He is my social grease. He is very understanding about the fact that I find social events and talking to people exhausting, and my need for quiet time.

THE MYERS-BRIGGS TYPES

First devised by US psychologists Katherine Cook Briggs and her daughter Isabel Briggs Myers, the Myers-Briggs test now runs to dozens of questions and 16 personality types, based on how we relate to the world and ourselves. Looking at the four broad questions below, are you more extroverted or introverted?

Are you focused inwards or outwards?	How do you prefer to absorb information?	How do you prefer to decide things?	How do you prefer to manage your life?
EXTROVERT I draw energy from outside stimulation.	**Sensing** I prefer the concrete and practical.	**Thinking** I prefer rationality and logic, valuing justice and fairness.	**Judging** I'm a planner who likes things organized.
INTROVERT I draw energy from within myself.	**Intuitive** I prefer the "big picture" and being imaginative.	**Feeling** I prefer connection and harmony, valuing empathy and forgiveness.	**Perceiving** I'm an improviser who likes things flexible.

> I'm extrovert, my partner is introvert. He helps me calm down, reflect, be less impulsive. We get cross with each other when I want to chat with the love of my life but he wants to read in total silence!

energy, a lot of conflicts can become a pattern of mutually supported needs. What looks antisocial and unfriendly may actually be a need to refresh oneself with some "me-time" or us-time. What looks restless may actually be a need to get some stimulation.

Successful "mixed" couples often make arrangements – Friday night is for vegging at home, Saturday night is party time. Whatever you decide, understanding how you work can make all the difference between frustration and satisfaction.

romance in subdued places, you may feel yourself a bit at a loss. Most usefully, the two terms can help you understand the dynamics between yourself and a date. Is the beautiful woman you met last week losing interest in you, or is she just tired because the party's been going on for hours? Is your new boyfriend bored with your company, or does he just need to get out and do something for a while? When you're aware and accepting of the different styles of

> My partner and I are both introverted, so it's important we each have our own time and space. We communicate openly about when each of us needs that space, and it works well.

Does it differ by gender?

Here's what the 1998 study by the Myers & Briggs Foundation found:

WOMEN

52.5%
extroverted

47.5%
introverted

MEN

45.9%
extroverted

54.1%
introverted

A LITTLE HELP FROM YOUR FRIENDS
PLATONIC LESSONS IN LOVE

Sometimes it can feel like everyone is coupled up except us – but even if that were true, our platonic relationships can help us to develop more secure attachment that may improve our next romance.

If you've ever poured out your sorrows to a close friend about a failed romance, or they've taken you out to cheer you up, you'll have experienced the soothing effect of friendship on a bruised heart.

Seeking a secure base
When a romance goes wrong and we feel the ache to be close again, that ache is our attachment system getting activated. As children, we feel upset if we get separated from our caregivers. That distress – our attachment system driving us to seek reconnection – is a powerful survival mechanism, pushing us back to the safety of their protection. As adults, our attachment system fires off when a romantic relationship falters, making us feel that nothing but reconnecting with our partner will cure our pain.

When we don't have a partner
If a relationship is over, though, or if we're in a spell of singledom, we have no "secure base" partner to turn to.

How, then, do we soothe ourselves? Rugged individualists might argue that we should just deal with it like adults, but human beings are social creatures and there's no shame in wanting connection: in fact, it's the healthiest thing for us. Our best bet is to turn to other people in our lives – close friends and family – and enjoy connecting with them. They can't be everything a partner is, but their love and attention can certainly help our attachment system to calm down.

Psychologists study attachment between parents and children and between lovers, but at other times in our lives, it's likely our attachment system will be occupied elsewhere. In 2010, Australian psychologist Ross B. Wilkinson found that adolescent attachments between best friends could be "complementary to the influence of parental attachments" – or, in lay terms, those whispered confidences or wild nights out could be just as important in shaping a person's expectations of romance as

their relationship with their family. As we move out of childhood, platonic relationships can shape us deeply, and we can use that closeness to help ourselves grow.

Humans at any age are creatures of community, and if we're too old to depend on a parent and don't have a long-term partner, then friends and family (and maybe religion) are the natural places for our attachment system to seek connection.

50%
A three-year **Swedish study** of over 13,600 people found that **having good friends decreased** the risk of having a **heart attack** by about **half.**

Friendly foundations

Seeking connection can be good in a crisis, but it's also good long term. If we have an insecure attachment style, contact with friends is actually a good way to practise feeling secure attachment in a safe environment.

Some friends may be more dependable than others, of course. A lonely phase can be a good time for a stock take on who makes you feel good and who doesn't, but the lower-key nature of friendship can be extremely useful. A friend won't want the commitment that worries an avoidant person, and doesn't have the heightened importance that flusters an anxious one.

If you can use time with your friends to address the basic fears of an insecure person – to prove to yourself that other people may, in fact, be willing and able to meet some of your needs – you may find that next time you meet someone, your subconscious mind will be better prepared for a loving relationship.

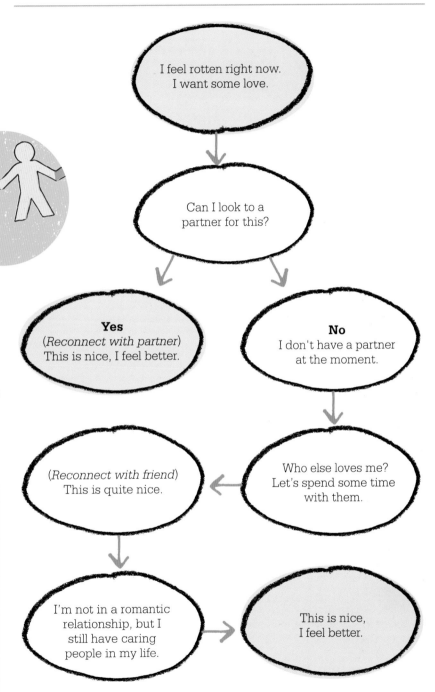

🔍 MICRO-MOMENTS OF LOVE

Love is just for lovers and close friends? Not according to North Carolina professor Barbara Fredrickson. In 2010, her research suggested that the condition of the vagus nerve, which helps us experience love and regulate our emotions, can be improved with regular loving-kindness meditation (see pages 56–57) but also by small everyday moments of connection with strangers. Share a smile in the street and your brain gets a small hit of love.

I feel rotten right now. I want some love.

Can I look to a partner for this?

Yes
(Reconnect with partner)
This is nice, I feel better.

No
I don't have a partner at the moment.

(Reconnect with friend)
This is quite nice.

Who else loves me? Let's spend some time with them.

I'm not in a romantic relationship, but I still have caring people in my life.

This is nice, I feel better.

THE PLATONIC CIRCUIT BREAKER

If we're having a difficult time and there's no partner available to make us feel better – or even if there is – friendship can be a great way to keep ourselves from going round and round the cycle of misery.

BE HONEST WITH ME

GETTING HELP FROM YOUR LOVED ONES

Sometimes it can be difficult to get a clear perspective on ourselves. If you're having trouble working out why you're single, a kind but truthful friend or relation can be a valuable mentor. If you've been looking for love for a while, it could be that you just happen not to have met the right person yet. But it could also be that by polishing your presentation, you can improve your chances that the right person will quickly spot you when they come along.

Find two friends of yours who know you well, who love you just the way you are, and who also have the social skills to know a good presentation when they see one. For preference, choose two people of your own generation, one of each sex. Then arrange to meet each one in turn, somewhere private, sit them down, and ask them to give you truthful, helpful feedback.

Now read on for ideas about which areas you might discuss, and how your mentor can most help you.

❓ LOOKING YOUR BEST

Helpful questions:

- Could you dress more flatteringly? For instance, are your clothes the right size and a good colour for you?
- Is your personal grooming all it could be? Is there a new hairstyle (or one you had before) that might suit you better?
- Could a different look showcase your personality better?

Don't forget:

You can't change your face, height, or build, so there's little to be gained from criticizing these. Maybe you could gain or lose some weight or put on some muscle, but that's a long-term project and dwelling on it right now may dent your confidence in the short-term. It could be as simple as taking more fresh air and vitamins to help you look healthier. Stick to things that you can change here and now.

❓ CARRYING YOURSELF WELL

Helpful questions:

- Is your body language friendly and appropriate? (See pages 112–115.)
- Do you have any habits, such as a nervous laugh or a fidget, that could put people off?
- Are you a good judge of how much personal space other people need?
- Is your posture generally confident and upright?

Don't forget:

You want to be appreciated for who you are, so there's no point trying to change your entire manner. Getting too self-conscious might only make things worse.

Instead, focus on how the way you're coming across may reflect inner discomfort. Then look for how you can feel better inside yourself; the way you come across will change along with that. (See pages 102–103 for exercises that should help.)

NEED SOME HELP?

Sit down with a close friend, ask for their opinion, and do your best to take it calmly!

Is there anything about my body language that puts people off?

Well, I suppose you chew your nails a lot.

Does it look that bad?

You tend to hunch up when you're doing it and look all stressed.

(Deep breath) Okay, thanks. Anything else?

---

⑦ YOUR ATTACHMENT STYLE

Helpful questions:

- Does your friend agree with you about what your attachment style is? (See pages 16–19.)
- Have they noticed whether you're prone to the same worries in different situations?
- What sort of attachment style do they think your previous partners have had? Is there a pattern there? (See pages 28–29.)
- If you want to feel more secure, can your friend work with you to support that? (See pages 34–35.)

Don't forget:

Whatever your attachment style, it is possible to have a good relationship with the right partner. An insecure style isn't a sentence to permanent singledom. Nor are attachment styles entirely distinct: everyone's a bit of a mix and that mix can change over time.

---

⑦ YOUR PAST

Helpful questions:

- Do you have unresolved issues that your friend thinks you could benefit from addressing?
- Do you have a habit of falling in love very quickly, or slowly? If so, should you adjust your expectations a bit? (See pages 130–131.)
- Does your friend think you remember past relationships fully, or can you be a bit selective?
- Are you vulnerable to a particular, unwise choice of partner? (See pages 28–29.)

Don't forget:

We can always grow and develop as people. A difficult past needn't mean a difficult future. Try to be open to change (see pages 32–33). Sometimes trying new habits can be hard – talk about how your friend can support you.

---

⑦ YOUR GOOD QUALITIES

Helpful questions:

- What's the first good thing that comes to mind when your friend thinks about you? (This could be either physical or in your manner.) Could you nurture it more? And how could you foreground it?
- When do you seem to have the most fun with others? (If you can increase those kinds of activities you'll be more likely to meet and attract others.)
- What are your talents? (Are you imaginative, insightful, witty, resourceful in a tight spot?) Can you use this to your advantage?

Don't forget:

Your friends and family love you for a reason! Improving your romantic presentation is as much about displaying those lovable qualities as it is about fixing the less lovable ones.

I ALWAYS GO FOR...

YOU AND YOUR TYPE

Does a particular kind of face always get your heart fluttering? Whether we mean to or not, we often read personality into features – knowing why can give us the power to choose our partners wisely.

What sort of face appeals to you? Do you like a face that's sweet and endearing? Glowering and Byronic? Sunny and open? Many of us have a particular "look" we go for; why is that? Some of it may have to do with past experiences. If, for instance, every red-haired person you've met has been particularly friendly and pleasant, on some level your brain may make the connection and you may start assuming that red hair indicates an outgoing personality. Some of it, though, is influenced by a series of other assumptions we make.

Looking for cues

While consciously we know we shouldn't judge a book by its cover, our brains are prone to make snap judgments when we see someone. We need to know how to behave towards them, so we immediately look for hints, pick up on anything that seems suggestive or familiar, and make some rapid assumptions – or overgeneralizations – about what to expect of their personality based on the style of their face. Studies suggest four big looks that lead us astray: the "babyface" look; an emotional cast to the face; a familiar look; and the "halo effect".

If you always seem to be excited by a certain kind of face, that may tell you something very useful – not just what you find physically attractive, but what kind of personality and relationship you are, deep down, on the watch for.

We can't change what we find attractive, of course – but the more we're aware of our subconscious reactions, the better we can be sure that we're judging with our hearts and our heads as well as our eyes.

BE MY BABY

Some features look more babyish than others. Big cues are:

- Round face
- Big cheeks
- Big forehead
- Small chin
- Button nose
- Fine eyebrows
- Big eyes (especially with big pupils)

How does that sound to you – unsexy, or adorable? We tend to associate faces like that with warmth, honesty, naivety, and submissiveness. We also tend to see them as "feminine" – perhaps because of an unwitting sexism, but also because the changes at puberty generally affect male faces more dramatically than female ones. (For example, men often develop heavier jawlines and brows.)

If you suspect you often go for big eyes and small features, you may be looking for a "sweetie" – someone lovable and trusting to cuddle with, and maybe to protect.

> Beauty is no quality in things themselves: it exists merely in the mind which contemplates them; and each mind perceives a different beauty.
>
> **David Hume,** philosopher, in *Of the Standard of Taste and Other Essays*, 1757

READING EMOTIONS

The six basic emotions of the human face are universal: happiness, fear, surprise, anger, disgust, and sadness look pretty much the same from the Australian Outback to the Arctic Circle. Because these emotions move our features into recognizable patterns, we tend to "see" certain emotions in faces that naturally match those patterns: someone with heavy brows and narrow lips, for instance, may register as mildly angry when their expression is actually neutral. Certain conclusions are all too easy to jump to:

- **"Angry"** features are associated with a forceful personality and limited warmth
- **"Sad", "fearful", or "surprised"** features are associated with being moderately warm but low in forcefulness
- **"Happy"** features are associated with high warmth and being confident rather than forceful
- **"Disgust"** features can be read as denoting negativity or pessimism, cynicism, and condescension.

Are you looking for someone warm and affectionate or strong and dynamic – or both? Also, take a look in the mirror: what emotions does your face tend to show? If they're not the emotions you want to convey, consider whether they reflect the emotions that you feel underneath – and perhaps want to change. A well-placed smile might help, too.

Happiness   **Disgust**

Surprise   **Anger**

Sadness   **Fear**

THE BIG SIX

There are some moods that everyone can recognize: in the 1970s, American psychotherapist Paul Ekman identified six "universal" facial expressions.

🔍 READING HORMONES

Certain features that signal genetic health are universally popular: symmetry, "averageness" (no feature too big or too small), and a clear complexion. We're less consistent with men than women. In women, "feminine" faces are usually preferred. In men, tastes vary: high-testosterone "masculine" faces are considered more virile but also more aggressive, while lower-testosterone men look "softer" and more nurturing.

»

THE HALO EFFECT

Some faces fit the template when it comes to good looks: symmetry, a clear complexion, bright eyes, and fine proportions shout out that this person is healthy and fertile, which appeals to our hormones.

What effect does this have on the owner of this face? Chances are, they've lived a life with the "halo effect": people have tended to give them the benefit of the doubt. Teachers have graded them more generously and made more excuses for any misbehaviour. At work, their chances of promotion may have been higher (unless they ran into a same-sex boss who felt their attractiveness to be a threat). They may even have received a lighter sentence if they committed a crime! None of this proves whether they're a bad or a good person, of course – just that they may have had a slightly different

In a 1991 study of small claims courts in the USA, **92 per cent of "mature-faced"** defendants who denied causing intentional harm were found to be at fault – but only **45 per cent of "baby-faced"** defendants.

🔍 YOU GET MY VOTE

Beauty can be powerful enough to rock democracy. A series of studies in the USA found that people presented with photos of unfamiliar politicians could guess their chances of electoral success with surprising accuracy – and even their margin of victory. Not only do people vote for candidates who "look good", but deep down we know it, too.

experience of life from the rest of us ordinary mortals. This experience may, in turn, make one person irresponsible and entitled but another person sociable and trusting – everyone is different.

What does it mean in the dating scene? If you happen to have a "perfect" face, that's good news for you as people will tend to grant you this "halo". If not, it's useful to be aware of it when you meet someone who does: just make sure that your assessment of their character is based on what they do, not how they look while they're doing it.

STRANGELY FAMILIAR

How do we react if a face looks familiar? In studies by Scottish researcher Lisa DeBruine, subjects were shown photographs of total strangers. When the faces were morphed by computers to increase their resemblance to the subject, they were rated more trustworthy – but also less sexy, perhaps because they looked like siblings or cousins. Faces morphed to look nothing like the subject were also rated as unattractive because they looked "untrustworthy" – too unfamiliar and we get wary, unless someone looks like another person we know we trust.

With our own faces, there's little we can do about this – we have no control over whether we look familiar to other people – but we might learn to think twice if we meet someone with a lovely personality but a face that we aren't quite sure about. Are your instincts right, or should you try a second date to see whether their face grows on you with familiarity?

🔍 THE LOOK OF LOVE

A study of 70 couples in the Netherlands in 2011 found that love does make a difference. Couples were asked to rate each other's looks, while members of the public also gave their honest opinion. Result? Compared with the general verdict, everyone rated their partner as more attractive than they really were. Once you're in someone's heart, it seems, you really are beautiful to them, no matter what anyone else thinks.

Body odour

The distinctly adult smell of body odour starts after puberty, in the sweat glands, and appears to act as a pheromone. Children sweat, too, but they don't get BO. Their "eccrine glands" release sweat directly onto the skin, as a cooling system. At puberty, our bodies also start using the "apocrine glands", which secrete sweat onto hair follicles and are stimulated not by heat but by adrenaline in times of stress and excitement – and that sweat includes chemicals like the androstenone, secreted by wild boars. Apocrine glands can get overactive during adolescence, but if we bathe regularly and wear clean clothes, our body odour can be an enticing pheromone.

Sniffing for a partner

Do we choose our partner with our nose? Perhaps more than we think. In 1995, a Swiss study at the University of Bern invited women to smell different men's used shirts, and found they preferred the smell of men whose immune systems differed genetically from their own. Non-identical immune systems produce, in theory, the healthiest offspring, and can be distinguished by chemical by-products that each have a unique smell – another invisible factor in the mating game.

So should we ditch the deodorant and put away the perfume? No, not necessarily: cleanliness is also a good indicator of health and wellbeing, and good grooming is attractive to most people. But if we get a bit sweaty, we might actually be engaging in a subconscious form of advertising – and when it comes to checking out potential mates, we might try closing our eyes and inhaling to see if this is someone our bodies want to get close to.

In 2009 American artist Judith Prays set up **"Pheromone Parties"**, where people selected blind dates by **smelling their T-shirts.** The organizers make no promises, but the idea went global.

10,000

Babies can smell their mother's milk, and parents can recognize their child's smell, but a **woman's sense of smell** is **10,000 times** more acute when ovulating.

A splash of attraction: Ladies, looking to dab on **something sultry** to attract a man? You may be wasting your time. The main "erotic" ingredient in perfumes is **musk**, and **women** have a **greater sensitivity** to it than men – **a thousand times** more sensitive, in fact. Your date probably won't smell it at all; the person getting turned on by the perfume will be you … but then again, if you're feeling sensual, you'll probably act sexier and get his attention that way.

x 1,000

5 million
scent receptors
10,000
different scents

Survival of the sniffiest: While we may not be the sharpest-nosed animals on the evolutionary tree – **humans** have about **5 million scent receptors**, but **dogs** have **220 million** – we can still distinguish around **10,000 different scents.** We use that ability not only to test our food, but also to check out the people around us, from parents to potential partners. **Newborn babies**, for instance, prefer to feed from an unwashed breast than a washed one, while **adults** can smell certain **musk odours** (pheromone smells that only matter when we're sexually mature) that pre-pubescent children can't identify at all.

SMILE PLEASE
THE BOND OF HUMOUR

Do you fall for people who make you laugh? If you meet someone attractive, do you try to amuse them? You may be shrewder than you realize: people's sense of humour tells us a lot about them.

A person who jokes with us wants to make us laugh – self-evident, perhaps, but important if we're trying to decide whether they'd make a good partner. An American study in 2009 found that an important element in humour is that it shows someone is interested in creating and maintaining social relationships: a person who starts with a joke is trying to get on the right foot with us, and a person who keeps us amused is making sure that they keep a positive connection with us. Someone who relates to us humorously may be a good romantic prospect simply because they're trying to get along with us.

Shared values
While we may all like a joke, we also want our partners to share our sense of humour. This may be more than just the desire to enjoy a laugh together: what we find funny says a lot about us. A study of 30 college couples in 1985 concluded that "shared humour reflects similar values and needs, resulting in consensual validation with an intimate other on how one perceives the world". In other words, when someone laughs at the same joke as you, you feel affirmed – you are agreeing happily together as to what is funny and what isn't.

If you feel uncomfortable with the kinds of joke a date tells, or with what they laugh at, it may signal something important: this person may have a worldview or beliefs that are incompatible with yours. One person's bad taste is another person's subversive joy, while one person's prudery is another's moral delicacy.

Of course, not everyone is a stand-up comedian, and there are plenty of lovable people who just can't tell a joke very well: being funny is not essential for romance. Instead, it's best to look at humour as a quick way of checking compatibility: see your date's reaction when tell the jokes you love most, and shrug off the pressure to laugh at a joke you don't like. The person you laugh with now may or may not be the person you hope to rejoice with later.

Do men always need to be the funny ones?
Maybe not. A study published in the *Journal of Psychology* in 2009 found that male and female subjects were rated as more attractive if they had a good sense of humour – but the men's ratings of the women jumped more than the women's ratings of the men.

Do witty women scare men off?
Not necessarily. In 1998 a study found that attractive women who made self-deprecating jokes were rated more highly by male subjects, because they seemed friendlier and more approachable.

> Oh dear, not funny – does it bother me?

> What kind of person tells that joke?

> Never mind, it's corny but cute.

WHAT DO YOUR JOKES SAY ABOUT YOUR VALUES?

Kind of humour	Defined as...	Kind of person
Wisecracks	Quickfire smart remarks	Intelligent, as this is hard to do well. May be a bit competitive, or trying to deflect discussion of their real feelings.
Deadpan	Straight-faced drollery	May be ironically bidding for intimacy, as the humour depends on you knowing that they're joking.
Broad humour	Naughty, "bathroom" jokes	Candid, unpretentious, earthy. Sometimes immature or aggressive.
Clowning	Physical fooling around	Physically assured, as this is a definite skill, though perhaps not comfortable in their own skin. Likes attention.
Raconteur	Holding the floor with funny stories	A performer who likes the spotlight. Observant, confident, and possibly prone to embroidering the truth.
Self-deprecating	Jokes at one's own expense	Can be opposite things: either a secure person who can take a laugh, or an insecure person bidding for reassurance.
Teasing	Jokes at the expense of someone else	Affectionate teasing can be proof of a bond. Someone whose jokes are always at other people's expense, though, may possess an innate sense of superiority.
Sarcasm	Biting and ironic	A person who can pull this off without sounding bitter or mean is probably quite subtle.
References	Pop culture quips and quotes	Cultured and/or geeky. If you like the same things, this can be great for bonding; if not, it can wear thin.
Parody	Send-ups and pastiches	Pay close attention to what and how they parody: it'll tell you a lot about what they consider foolish.
Dark	Gallows or tasteless humour	May suggest someone who likes to push at boundaries – or someone who has learned to live with their own misfortune.

WISHING ON A STAR

WHEN YOU NEED TO LISTEN TO YOURSELF

It's easy to laugh at people who consult horoscopes or fortune-tellers about their romantic prospects, but even if this is simply a superstitious habit, it may reveal something unexpected – if we look at it the right way.

Many of us don't believe in fortune-telling, but most of us could confess to the occasional moment when we sneakily read our horoscope and feel a little twinge of hope if it tells us that we might meet a beautiful stranger. Similarly, when we take a personality quiz online, we hope to be told we're like Jane Eyre or Mr Darcy. Why are we drawn to these things even if we don't quite take them seriously?

> We've got something for everyone.

Roll up, folks

Circus maestro P.T. Barnum used to claim, "We've got something for everyone", and for that grand claim he earned his name in the annals of psychology. The "Barnum effect" – or the "Forer effect", after the American psychologist who identified the phenomenon – describes our tendency to see ourselves in neutral statements. Write a description that could apply to almost anyone, and people will almost always assume it applies to them in particular.

In 1948, Bertram R. Forer gave his students a personality test that would supposedly offer each of them an individual analysis. (Try some of the test yourself, opposite.) In fact, they all got the same result – but because the statements were so general, they gave it an average rating of 4.26 out

33%

An estimated **33 per cent** of Americans **believe in astrology – 75 per cent** of them are **women**.

SEE YOURSELF IN THIS?

Here are some of the statements in Forer's personality test – how well do they describe you (and everyone else)?

- You have a great need for other people to like and admire you.

- You have a tendency to be critical of yourself.

- You have a great deal of unused capacity which you have not turned to your advantage.

- While you have some personality weaknesses, you are generally able to compensate for them.

- At times you have serious doubts as to whether you have made the right decision or done the right thing.

- At times you are extroverted, affable, sociable, while at other times you are introverted, wary, reserved…

 ## HOW DO YOU FEEL ABOUT YOURSELF?

1 **Find an online horoscope, preferably one that focuses on your love life.**

2 **Every day for a week, read your forecast once, copy-paste the text somewhere, and save it. Don't reread.**

3 **At the end of the week, without looking at your saved forecasts, write down what you remember it told you about yourself and your love life.**

4 **Go back to the actual forecasts, and compare them with what you've remembered.**

Are you looking at your romantic future? Probably not. But your notes do show your romantic expectations. As these shape our behaviour, there may be hints to your future there.

5 **The following week, try the same exercise. This time, make an effort to remember only the positive forecasts. You may find your confidence increases.**

If you feel you're living under an unlucky star, this exercise can be a good way to see if the jinx really lies in your selective observations. Better still, make a list of the positive forecasts and carry it with you as an extra boost to your confidence.

of 5 – or 85.2 per cent – for accuracy. Forer's experiment shows we have a tendency to "subjective validation" – assuming something is right if it seems to relate to us.

Horoscopes, too, are supposed to be personally tailored to us (and it's hard to resist the feeling of individual attention). In a classroom experiment, students were given a list of yesterday's horoscopes and asked to choose which sounded most accurate for them. Students in the control group, who weren't told which prediction related to which star sign, compared the predictions yesterday with their experiences today and tended to pick the best match, while students who were given the star signs as well were far more likely to go for "their" horoscope: Virgos chose Virgos, Scorpios chose Scorpios, and so on. Although they already knew how their day had panned out, they were still swayed by the classifications.

So are we just dupes?

While we may see ourselves in neutral statements that could apply to anyone, it's still worth thinking about what we see. As shown on pages 32–33, we have a tendency to be selective about what we notice. If we feel good about ourselves, we remember luck and compliments; if we feel bad, criticism and misfortune – and we have a tendency to seek out the company of people who validate our positive or negative self-image.

If you've ever read your horoscope, ask yourself this: what do you mainly remember it saying about you? In other words, presented with a "Barnum statement", what jumps out at you? We may not see our future in a crystal ball. What we might see is our own self-image looking back at us – and that image can shape our future decisions. Your reactions to a general statement are a foreshadowing of your reaction to meeting new people. Once you understand your own reactions, you may have a clearer picture of where your self-image or confidence needs a boost – to help with that, try the simple exercises above. That way, when you do meet a beautiful stranger, you'll be ready for them.

GIVE YOURSELF A BREAK

COPING WITH THE LONELY TIMES

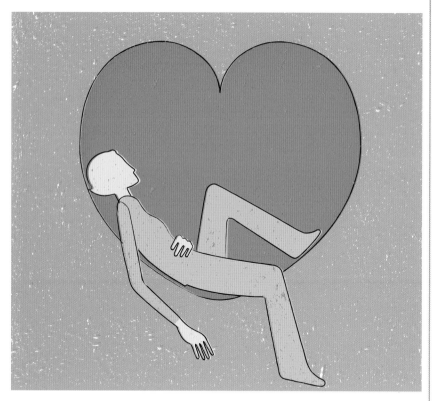

However psychologically ready for a relationship we are, sometimes we just haven't found the right person yet. How do we get through a spell of being single without losing our confidence?

Sometimes, what we really need in life is compassion and understanding. We want that from a partner – but if a partner isn't to be had just now, there's no reason to suffer in the meantime. An important psychological skill we can develop is what American therapist Kristin Neff calls "self-compassion": the art of nurturing ourselves.

Self-compassion

All of us can be hard on ourselves. If we feel down about ourselves, we tend to jump to the conclusion that there's something wrong with us. Rather than acknowledge how we feel, we look for reasons – as if we have to find an explanation for our sadness in faults that we have to fix before we can feel better again.

Searching for reasons can also create conflict with others, whether we're single or dating. If we feel angry, for instance, we may rush from the emotion to the reaction. Thoughts and plans will start bubbling up: "He's such a pain", "I know I'm right about this", "What can I say to put him in his place?" If our minds rush us straight through to attack mode like this, we risk communicating the reaction to our feeling – "You're an idiot!" – rather than the feeling itself – "I feel angry with you right now."

We don't help ourselves by running at this pace. We need love and kindness, but the first person who must give it to you is yourself. (See overleaf for some exercises to help develop this ability.)

Mindfulness

Psychologists nowadays are taking an increasing interest in the Buddhist practice of "mindfulness". Put simply, this is the practice of letting ourselves be gently aware of whatever thoughts and feelings we are experiencing –

not forming judgments about them or committing to them, just observing and accepting that they're there.

Romantic relationships often involve difficult emotions, whether it's the stress of a quarrel with your partner or the nerve-racking cycle of hope, disappointment, and discouragement that can go with searching the dating scene for someone to be with. If we've been looking for love for a while, the more painful feelings can start to turn into opinions: "I'm such a loser", "I must be ugly", "All the good partners are already taken." If instead we can sit with these thoughts and accept them for what they are – I feel insecure, I feel sad, I feel lonely – then they become much easier to calm.

happiest when we can accept and trust our own reactions, strengths, and weaknesses, when we are able to assess ourselves and our experiences candidly, when we act in accordance with our values and character, and when we are open and honest with the people we love.

While it can be tempting to push away knowledge of our own flaws and weaknesses, in the long term

we're actually more secure if we accept them: our weaknesses won't destroy us, but trying to deny them leaves us in conflict with ourselves and with our real experiences. If we can be honest with ourselves and others, and act according to our honest understanding, we won't live without bad times – no one does – but we will have a foundation of self-respect to rest upon.

> Just bringing people's awareness to their true self-concept increases their sense of meaning in life.
>
> **Rebecca J. Schlegel, Joshua A. Hicks, Jamie Arndt, and Laura A. King** University of Missouri

Authenticity

The best way to keep our self-esteem stable is to base it on an authentic "self-concept" – that is, a mental image of ourselves that is reasonably realistic. Social psychologists and authenticity experts Brian Goldman and Michael Kernis identify four key components: awareness, "unbiased processing", behaviour, and "relational orientation". To put this in less technical terms: we are at our

LET YOURSELF FEEL
It can be hard to accept painful emotions; sometimes it feels like they'll overwhelm us if we don't tamp them down. Even so, it is possible – and often helpful – to take some comfort in accepting them.

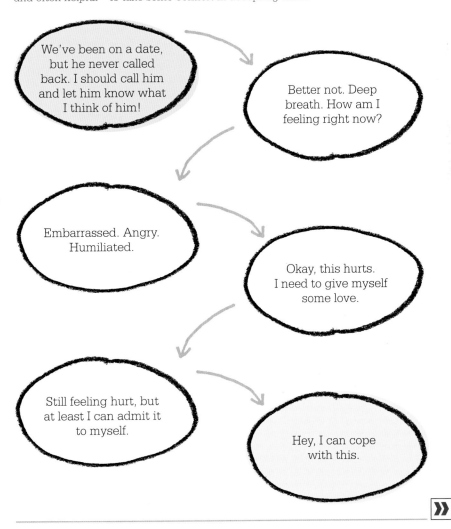

>> Practising self-compassion

When we become sympathetically aware of our own feelings – when we are compassionate and mindful – they are much less likely to trip us up. We all want love, but the one person who has been in your life from the beginning and will be there to the end is you. A constant companion should be a kind companion. It's not always easy to treat ourselves compassionately; try some exercises to help you along. With practice, you will find yourself better able to cope with time alone – and that can only help in the ongoing search for love.

🪷 KEEP IN TOUCH WITH YOURSELF

Sometimes we just need to steady ourselves. Julia Cameron's book, *The Artist's Way*, focuses on how to remain creative and productive without turning to unhealthy habits or feeling one must be tormented in order to be imaginative. In it she recommends "morning pages". First thing each day, sit down and write out three pages longhand – three pages of anything, be it nonsense, a list of chores, or your deepest fears. The point is simply to keep the pen moving and listen to yourself. This way, you start the day by clearing your head with a writing meditation. You may not be a working artist, but we all use creativity to solve our problems every day, and the more comfortable we are with letting our thoughts flow, the better balanced we feel as the day goes on.

🪷 MINDFUL BREATHING

1 **Get yourself somewhere physically comfortable –** preferably sitting up, so that you don't fall asleep. Close your eyes and relax.

2 **Let yourself become aware of the sensations in your body** – the air on your skin, the seat under you, your feet in your shoes. Thoughts will drift in and out of your mind; don't worry about that. Just let them come and go, and keep returning your attention to your sensations.

3 **Move your focus to the sensation of your breath.** Feel the rhythm of it going in and out. Don't try to speed it up or slow it down; let it happen comfortably.

4 **Focus on a particular place in your body where you feel your breath most directly.** Many people like to focus on the nose, feeling the place where the air enters and leaves their body, but if you prefer to concentrate on your throat, chest, or stomach, go with what pleases you at that particular moment.

This is an excellent meditation for calming yourself, and it's also perfect for letting your emotions untangle. If strong feelings arise, let them happen: you may find that the chance to observe them in safety makes them much easier to deal with.

🪷 LOVING-KINDNESS MEDITATION

1 **Find a comfortable place to sit, then close your eyes, and relax.** Focus on your breathing for a little while to help yourself settle down.

2 **Focus your attention on yourself,** and start encouraging a feeling of loving kindness, accepting yourself as a person of inherent worth. Try repeating phrases in your mind such as: "May I be well," "May I be safe," and "May I be happy." This can feel a bit odd at first – if you like, adapt the phrases to make them closer to the way you naturally talk – or try the next step and then come back to this one.

3 **Think of someone you're fond of,** preferably not a romantic partner but a close friend or relative. Direct your feelings of loving kindness towards them.

4 **Move your attention to someone neutral to you,** someone you neither like nor dislike. Try to feel loving kindness towards them, too, in recognition of your shared humanity.

5 **If you're feeling up to it, think about someone you find difficult to like,** wishing them well even if you personally don't care for them.

You can also extend this to all humanity, or, if you're having a hard day, limit the number of people you cultivate loving kindness towards. As a regular practice, this exercise can be amazingly good at helping you feel more at ease in the world.

 CREATE AN INNER COMFORTER

All of us know what it's like to have an "inner critic": the voice in our heads telling us in merciless detail everything wrong with what we do, think, feel, and are. It may seem like it's for your own good, but that critic is not your friend – would you be friends with an actual person who talked to you like that?

What we can do instead is cultivate a compassionate self, a voice that doesn't blame but encourages. If the habitual message of the inner critic is "Well, you really made a fool of yourself there, didn't you?" the message of the compassionate self is "I love you and I don't want you to suffer."

Several times each day, stop and try to hear this inner compassionate voice. Let other kind phrases follow the one above – "I forgive you," "You can do this," "You'll be okay," "I love you." Most of us aren't used to talking to ourselves in this way, but you'll probably find that you start to like this new voice once you're listening out for it.

Sometimes we fear that by loving ourselves too much we'll drive away the love of others. Vanity and arrogance do that, perhaps, but those are inverted insecurity, not real love: they depend on feeling better than other people, as if that's the only way to avoid feeling inferior. Real self-love, on the other hand, draws in the love of others: it creates an inner warmth and stability that sustains people – above all ourselves.

SOFTEN, ALLOW, SOOTHE

How do we first feel an emotion? Usually as a physical sensation. Try this exercise to help yourself deal with difficult feelings.

1　**Sit and relax for a while,** perhaps using some mindful breathing to centre yourself.

2　**Soften.** Become aware of where your body is experiencing the emotion, such as a tight throat or an aching heart. Try to picture a warm, calming sensation there. Imagine a softening of the pain rather than trying to get rid of it. Give yourself some physical compassion.

3　**Allow.** Accept that the feeling is there; don't rush to push it away. You're feeling something difficult; it won't destroy you. Your mind doesn't have to come up with an instant solution. Give yourself some mental compassion.

4　**Soothe.** Give yourself some loving kindness. Treat yourself as you'd treat a friend you loved; you wouldn't tell them they were a loser for feeling bad. Give yourself some emotional compassion, empathizing with your own distress and wishing you could ease the pain.

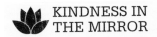 KINDNESS IN THE MIRROR

When we look in the mirror, too often we're only checking for faults. We see the pimples or the wrinkles, the too-big this and the too-small that. In effect, we're looking for reasons why someone wouldn't like us.

Instead, try this: every morning before you get showered, shaved, or made up – when you're at your most natural, ungroomed self – stand before the mirror and look into your own eyes. Using your own name, say aloud ten times, "[My name], I love you exactly the way you are."

Don't rush this exercise; even if you do it slowly it won't take much time. You may be surprised at the depth of emotion it throws up, but keep doing it. Love yourself exactly the way you are, and make sure your brain hears your voice saying it.

🔍 HAVE A LAUGH

"Laughter is the best medicine", as the old saying goes, but there's science behind it, too: a study by the Royal Society found that subjects who watched comedians showed a significantly higher pain threshold than those who watched a documentary. Since we feel the pain of social rejection in the same centres of our brains that register physical pain, a good laugh can be more than just a temporary distraction: it can give our nervous systems a positive boost that helps our all-round wellbeing.

CHAPTER 2
THE
SEARCH
FINDING THE RIGHT PERSON FOR YOU

ON THE LOOKOUT
GETTING OUT THERE

There are many popular ways to meet someone, which we'll cover later in this chapter. First, though, what are your comfort zones? If you have a clear idea, you'll probably feel happier about putting yourself out there.

All of us have our happy places, and what they are can say a lot about us. It's too much to hope that the love of one's life will simply wander into a favourite café one day, but precisely because finding romance usually involves more active "getting out there" to look for Mr or Ms Right, we're much better off if we have a clear idea about what kind of "out there" we're happy getting into.

There's no point making the search for romance feel punishing. If you really can't stand certain places or experiences, then the chances are that anyone you meet there wouldn't suit you either. Better, probably, to ask yourself what sort of activities and environments feel right for you.

Physical comfort zones

We're sometimes advised to join a sports club or a choir if we want to meet someone new, but that can sound a bit simplistic. Another way to look at it is this: what sorts of places and activities make you feel good? Where are you relaxed? What kinds of social setting let you express yourself freely?

Questions like that can help us clarify what we're looking for in a partner. Suppose you love going to soccer matches: the energy of the crowd and the thrill of suspense are the high point of your week. Now, a hectic stadium might not be the best place to meet someone, and the best person for you might not be the biggest soccer fan. What you might decide, though, is that you're looking for someone who shares your love of excitement and will join you in the rough-and-tumble side of life. Looking at it that way immediately broadens your options.

Psychological comfort zones

Another question: what do you value? What qualities would you say were the bedrock of your identity?

(Try the Happiness Pie opposite.) In answering this question, it's important not to conflate "What's central to my identity" with "What I spend most of my time doing": focus on the aspects of life that make you feel your best, healthiest, fullest self.

When it comes to looking for love, it's wise to seek out partners who will support and encourage our finest qualities. This technique can help you decide what to prioritize. We none of us have all the free time we could wish, and most of us can't do all the extra-curricular stuff we'd like. When you can identify what your most important values are, that should give you some pointers: if you have to choose between activities, give the most time to the ones that most reflect who you want to be. We all want someone who loves us for who we really are, so your choices need to be realistic – pick things that make you the best version of yourself rather than trying to turn into someone else. If you can do that, it improves your chances of finding someone who harmonizes with your aspirations – and, of course, will make your life feel more meaningful in its own right.

✏ THE HAPPINESS PIE

American psychologist Michael Frisch suggests a useful exercise for determining your life goals and values. Draw a circle. This is your "pie", and you're going to divide it into "slices" showing how much time and effort you put into each aspect of your life. The pie below is just one example.

1 To begin with, draw your **"real version" pie:** this is how much time and energy you currently put into the different aspects of your life.

2 Now draw another circle, this time the **"ideal version".** This is how important each of these aspects really is to you: how much of yourself do you want to be putting into each aspect?

3 When you've marked the **difference between your real and ideal pies,** think about ways in which you could try to bring the real pie closer to the ideal one. If you can find activities that develop certain aspects and also put you in the way of meeting new people, your chances of finding interesting new dates could improve a lot.

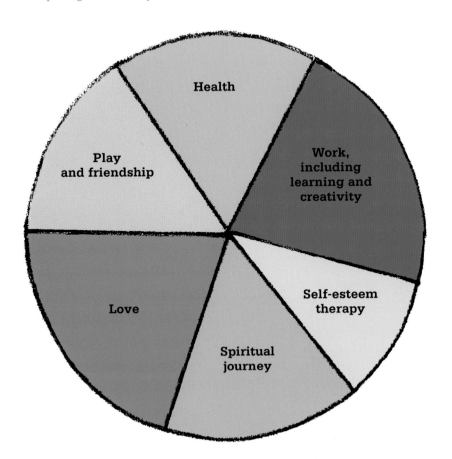

🔍 WHAT'S YOUR COMFORT ZONE?

When you hang out in your favourite places, what is it that appeals to you? A good partner for you might not like the exact same places, but they might like the same experiences that draw you there, such as…

EXCITEMENT

PHYSICAL CHALLENGE

SOLITUDE

SKILL-BASED ACTIVITY

DOMESTICITY

SENSORY PLEASURE
(FOOD, SPAS, ETC.)

CROWDS

ARTISTIC INSPIRATION

INTELLECTUAL CHALLENGE

A SENSE OF HISTORY

NATURE

A SENSE OF COMMUNITY

ENTERTAINMENT

HEY WORLD, I'M AVAILABLE!

SENDING OUT THE RIGHT SIGNALS

When it comes to meeting new people, we all want to come across well. How do we find ways of presenting ourselves well without becoming too self-conscious or coming across as too eager?

How guarded do you feel when it comes to finding love? It's healthy to be a little cautious: giving someone your heart is a major decision, and leaping into love on short acquaintance can cause heartache later. On the other hand, wanting a relationship is more or less a prerequisite of getting into one: if a person really doesn't care about having a relationship, they tend to stay single. How do we get a healthy perspective on what we want?

Checking your signals

Sometimes our fears lead us to give the wrong impression. If we hide what we really think, for instance, we'll only attract someone who likes the fake us, not the real us. Or maybe we overcompensate: someone who is afraid their "strong personality" will alienate people often becomes more confrontational, just to test whether people can "accept me for who I am". Or maybe we want to be accepted despite our insecurities, and so we cross the line from being self-deprecating to becoming a real downer to be with.

55%

Body language is thought to make up about **55 per cent of communication.** Get **at ease in your body,** and you're more than halfway there.

GET INTO YOURSELF

The best way to act and feel desirable is to enjoy your own body, even when there's no one else there. To get into the mood with yourself, try some of these suggestions:

✔ Listen to music with a sensuous rhythm. Maybe even dance to it just to enjoy feeling yourself sway.

✔ Enjoy the aromas of incense, scented candles, essential oils, or other good-smelling things. Appreciate inhaling delicious air. You might like to pair this with the mindful breathing meditation on page 56.

✔ Take a long bath or power shower. Don't just hurry to get clean: experiment with different temperatures, and really enjoy the feeling of water on your skin.

✔ Get comfortable touching your own body. If there are any parts of you you're self-conscious about, try a loving-kindness meditation from page 56, focusing on the sensations you feel there and sending warm, affectionate energy in that direction. If it's part of you, it's valuable.

I am lovable.

Work on remembering that you're a valid, lovable person (see pages 54–55 for help with that). You may also want to ask a trusted friend whether you overemphasize any aspects about yourself that worry you (see pages 40–41) – they'll probably say there's nothing to worry about, but if you do turn out to be doing something off-putting, it's not the end of the world. A habit is just that – a habit, not the key to our identity. Throughout our lives, we all pick up and discard different ways of behaving, and they don't have to say very much about us if we don't let them.

Do we need flirting school?
Often dating advice encourages us to focus on how we're coming across to other people. The problem with focusing purely on what we should say or do in order to send the right message is that when we're self-conscious, our anxiety levels climb. An encounter that might be a sparky getting-to-know-you conversation becomes a test of our performance skills: no one is at their best when they add stage-fright to the mix. A better approach might be to focus on your own desires. Try some of the suggestions above and right – when you feel relaxed and at ease in your body, flirtation can flow naturally from attraction rather than being a skill you have to work at.

None of us can be sure that we're coming across perfectly, and we probably aren't. If you can move the focus to feeling good in yourself, though, then the image you present to the world will be relaxed and attractive because that's how you feel. The best way to seem like a desirable person, ultimately, is to enjoy being you.

SENSUOUS WALKING MEDITATION

Ever noticed that some people can set the air sizzling just by walking down the street? There's no magic to it; these people are just taking a sensuous pleasure in the feeling of their bodies in motion. Try it: soon you'll be sending out the right signals effortlessly.

1 **Go somewhere that feels peaceful and safe, such as a park.** Wear comfortable shoes and clothes: this is for your own pleasure, not a performance.

2 **As you walk, start a mindfulness meditation** (see page 56). Feel the ground beneath your feet, the rhythm of your legs, the swing of your hips. Don't try to change them, just focus on how they naturally feel.

3 **Start cultivating a feeling of sensory delight.** Focus on the areas of your body that feel most pleasurable. This doesn't have to be traditionally sexy parts of you: if the sun is warm on your forehead or your long, woolly socks feel great on your calves, enjoy that.

4 **Repeat one or two phrases in your head that help you feel attractive** – "Hey, beautiful!" or "Looking good there!" If this feels a little silly, enjoy laughing at yourself: no one else can see inside your head, after all, and a bit of silliness never hurt anyone.

5 **Carry on walking along,** experiencing your own sensuous rhythm and feeling as gorgeous as possible.

LET YOUR BODY TELL YOU YOU ARE POWERFUL AND DESERVING, AND YOU BECOME MORE PRESENT, ENTHUSIASTIC, AND AUTHENTICALLY YOURSELF

AMY CUDDY, SOCIAL PSYCHOLOGIST AND ASSOCIATE PROFESSOR, HARVARD BUSINESS SCHOOL

WE MET ON THE BUS

THE CHANCE ENCOUNTER

Sometimes, it seems, fate just drops a person into our path. If we run across someone wonderful – on the bus or wherever we happen to be – what's the smart way to act on instant attraction?

According to the 16th-century English poet and playwright Christopher Marlowe, love is a question of fate and strikes us in the first moment. While that may be poetic licence, it's true that we tend to notice at once if someone's attractive, and if we're going to feel comfortable with someone, we often "click" quickly.

> Where both deliberate, the love is slight: / Whoever loved, that loved not at first sight?
>
> **Christopher Marlowe**
> from *Hero and Leander*, 1598

Love at first sight?

When it comes to chance meetings, our attachment style (see pages 16–19) affects how quickly we jump from "I like the look of you" to "I love you." People towards the anxious end of the attachment spectrum are the most prone to falling in love at short notice: if we worry about rejection and think of others as better than us (see pages 22–23), we have a strong need for caring and acceptance, which can turn to yearning on relatively short acquaintance. Avoidant people, on the other hand, are the least prone to love at first sight: any kind of commitment can feel uncomfortable, and distance is something avoidants prefer to maintain. Anxious people find it hardest to keep their emotions on an even keel, so a sudden attraction to someone can be overwhelming. For an avoidant person, keeping emotions tamped down is a lifelong habit – they may feel attracted at first sight, but the move from attraction to love is something they would generally rather avoid. Secure people are somewhere in the middle: they're as prone as anyone else to be struck by someone's charm, but they tend to feel you need to build intimacy before you can really say you're in love.

Thinking with your head

It's worth remembering we're all prone to attributing good qualities of character to someone who is good-looking. This "halo effect" (see pages 42–44) can turn our heads, so we need to keep that in mind even when our hearts are fluttering.

If you do meet someone on the bus or any other random place, there's a pressure to act quickly: if you don't ask them out now, you may never meet again. This throws a lot of us off balance – one reason why it's good to keep our self-esteem in good order (see pages 34–35). It's also good to be confident about the basic moves and social skills that go with being unthreatening (see right) – the last thing you want is to scare someone off. Asking out a stranger is taking a chance, and should only be done if you're already chatting – asking someone out without talking to them first can look a bit weird – but there are happy couples who meet this way, so there's no harm in you trying. After all, if they don't know you, at least they can't embarrass you by telling all your friends if they turn you down.

The odds of meeting the perfect person unexpectedly are longer than the odds if you actively seek out opportunities, but it can happen. The trick is to keep your head as much as possible: that way you're better placed to come across well if it does happen, and then to keep on an even keel.

 ## BEST MOVES FOR A CHANCE ENCOUNTER

Whether it's a man or a woman who's caught your eye, here are some tips for getting it right:

✔ **Observe their body language.** "Closed" signals, such as turning away from you or holding a book up as a barrier, mean they're not interested; watch instead for the people who turn towards you and leave their arms relaxed.

✔ **Start with a non-sexual comment.** "You're gorgeous" is coming on too strong; "Nice hat" or "I read that book, what do you think of it?" are much better ways to start a conversation.

✔ **Ask their opinions about things.** That shows you're interested in them as a person, not just a body, and lets you find out how they think.

✔ **If you're getting along and you'd like to see more of them, be direct.** "I'd really like to ask you out; would you be interested?" shows them you're confident, and lets them tell you straight out if the answer's yes or no. If it's a yes, accept whatever level of contact they're prepared to offer, follow up soon, and meet somewhere public.

⊗ TIPS FOR THE GUYS

There are some places where even if a woman seems wonderful, it's not a great idea to approach her. Women are, on the whole, more alert for their physical safety, and with good reason. Here are some places where you should think carefully about trying your luck:

✖ **Enclosed spaces, such as elevators and empty train carriages.** If she can't make a quick getaway, she'll feel wary.

✖ **Isolated places.** Without any witnesses, she's without protection. This includes being in a lonely room at a party: if she wants to get back to her friends, don't try to stop her.

✖ **On the street.** If she's got somewhere to be, she'll be annoyed if you don't respect that.

✖ **First meetings in a workplace.** It's one thing to flirt with a colleague, but if a woman's there to give a presentation or hand over an order, remember: her career depends on giving a good impression. Making it harder for her to do her job is a turn-off.

✖ **Very drunken gatherings.** A gentleman doesn't take advantage.

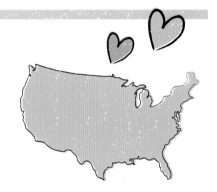

51%

Like the look of someone? **51 per cent** of Americans say **flattery** is the **best way to attract** someone. (Just don't be too cloying.)

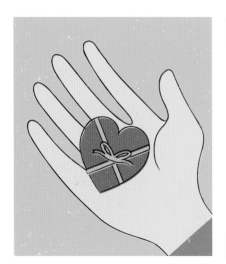

I LIKE YOU, BUT...
IS FRIENDSHIP ALL THAT'S ON OFFER?

Sometimes the liking runs both ways, but maybe the attraction is all on your side. If we don't ask, we may never be sure. If we find ourselves having romantic feelings for a friend, what's the next step?

If you feel attracted to a friend, it may be that they're feeling the same for you. Whether to take the plunge and ask is a big decision in a friendship: the fear of "ruining things" keeps many a lover quiet.

To speak or not to speak?

Realistically, of course, there is a chance of rejection, and different friendships can absorb that impact to different degrees. There are risks in staying quiet too, though – some more serious than others. If you never declare your love to a friend who actually might be interested in you too, you may both miss out, but you can stay friends and move on to other people. On the other hand, if you keep quiet and hope the friendship will somehow some day turn into something more, you're probably distracting yourself from pursuing love elsewhere. If you're caught in this trap, try the exercises opposite to help clear your thoughts about what to do.

If it's definitely one-sided

Perhaps you might be attracted to a friend who's clearly not interested: they're happily involved with someone else, they've dropped hints to that effect, or you just know you're not their type. What then?

It's important not to get caught up in the pursuit-withdrawal dynamic, in which frustration leads to obsession and misery (see pages 148–149). Giving up on a hope of love is always painful, but so too is hanging on to a hope that won't be fulfilled. Work on directing your attention elsewhere, so you can move past the unhappiness.

Unrequited crushes on a friend aren't necessarily all bad. True, they may never want to be with you romantically, but you can take some things from the friendship that may help you in your search for someone who does return your feelings. First: if you can identify what it is about this person that draws you, it may help you clarify what you're looking for in a romantic partner.

Second: the fact this person likes you is a sign that you have qualities an attractive person values. Maybe this individual doesn't want more than friendship, but there are other people like them out there who probably will.

Unrequited love can be painful, there are no two ways about it. If we can keep ourselves from getting trapped in it, though, there are good things to be gained. Remember that if one attractive person likes your company, probably other attractive people will, too.

> ...it's wicked to throw away all your gifts because you can't have the one you love.
>
> **Amy March**
> in the *Little Women* series
> by Louisa May Alcott

DO I DECLARE MYSELF?

1 When we're in the throes, it can be hard to decide what to do about romantic feelings for a friend: the possible good and bad outcomes of declaring yourself can be confusing. To help you clarify your thoughts, try this simple flow chart:

YES

Best-case scenario
They want you, too. Hooray!

Worst-case
They say no, and it causes problems in the friendship.

NO

Best-case scenario
You stay friends, you get over your feelings, and you eventually meet someone else.

Worst-case
You keep hoping friendship will turn into love, but never say anything, stuck in an obsessive longing.

2 Take a pen and paper and list what reasons there might be for each of the outcomes above. If you think it would cause problems in the friendship if you declared yourself, try using a chart like this one:

IF I TAKE THE PLUNGE

It could cause problems because...	Do I think these problems are likely?	Are there any ways I could head them off?	Are there any drawbacks to those solutions?	If so, how could I make myself feel better?
He/she will doubt I ever really valued their friendship.	Yes. I always hoped it would turn into something more.	I'd have to stress that I value our friendship nonetheless.	I might not be believed.	I'd have to brace myself for the friendship cooling.
It might be awkward hanging out alone together.	Yes.	If I hung back for a while, we might get back to normal.	If we don't get back to normal, I'd miss them and feel lonely.	I could plan to spend time with other friends who value me.
Our other friends might think I've gone too far.	No, I'm probably being a bit paranoid.	I could assure them that I'll understand if his/her answer is no.	I might still make a fool of myself.	I could share this with the friends I think would be supportive.

3 When you've completed this chart, you may still decide that the best choice is to say nothing and keep the friendship as it is. If so, you may have to let go of your romantic hopes for this particular relationship and start directing them towards new people.

ACROSS A CROWDED OFFICE
THE PROS AND CONS OF DATING AT WORK

We spend most of our waking hours at work, and we usually have a lot in common with our colleagues. The odds of liking a colleague are high, but are workplace romances really worth the trouble?

When you take a chance on love in the workplace, it's not just your heart on the line but your livelihood as well. Unlike most romances, you can't just "separate" if things go wrong: you have to keep working together. Not only does this raise the stakes between you, but it also tends to create pressure from third parties: your other colleagues may well have plenty of opinions about what your relationship really means. How, then, do you manage things if you and a colleague seem made for each other?

Keeping in with co-workers

One of the great worries of a workplace romance is the fear of antagonizing other colleagues. If you're dating someone higher up the corporate ladder, you may well be right: in 2012, an American study of 212 workers found that not only do the majority assume that a colleague dating "up" is driven more by career motives than by love, but they are also less likely to trust and share information with that colleague. Even if you have no intention of passing anything on, fellow workers might not be willing to take the chance. Another American study of 297 people in 1998 found that female colleagues were more likely to be suspicious than male ones. You may need to tread carefully to prove that you're not a spy in their midst!

On the positive side, the same study found that people dating a colleague felt better about their own job performance, and tended to feel particularly loving towards their partner when work was going well. If you can navigate wary colleagues, a successful working romance can be a virtuous circle of improved work and improved love.

✎ SEXUAL HARASSMENT IN THE WORKPLACE

Is someone making unwelcome eyes at you? Interested in someone but don't want to be creepy? Psychologists William E. Foote and Jane Goodman-Delahunty divide sexual harassment into three categories:

1 **"Misperceiving harassers":** people who don't mean any harm but can be a bit clueless when it comes to separating professional friendliness from romantic interest and understanding when it is inappropriate to hit on someone.

2 **"Exploitative harassers":** aggressive individuals – including men more likely to be rapists – who are carrying dangerous attitudes into the workplace because they're dangerous people.

3 **"Misogynistic harassers":** men who resent women in the workplace and use sexism to make them uncomfortable, especially in "boys' club" environments. Women sometimes do this to male colleagues, too, but only if it's a mostly female workplace.

Recognizing these types of harassment and which one you're dealing with can help you know whether to treat a problem as an unwanted courtship or as a deliberate threat.

Limiting the fallout

Most relationships end eventually, as colleagues will probably be quick to remind you, so what do you do if that happens? A lot will probably depend on how well you've maintained your working relationships with your team: if you've done your best to prove trustworthy during the romance, you'll be less expected to cause problems if it ends.

A lot will also depend how cleanly you can end the relationship. When deciding whether to date, this is a situation where it's particularly important to ask yourself whether this person can handle frustration and embarrassment well – because there'll be plenty of that for both of you along the way and you don't want to get the blame.

Ultimately, the decision comes down to weighing up the risks and the advantages, which will vary from individual to individual. The wisest course is to be as honest and mature as possible and hope for the best.

How many peope date at work? Estimates are high, ranging from **47 per cent** in the US Office Romance Survey by Vault.com in 2003 to a heady **79 per cent** at a large UK law firm in 2002.

In a study at Stanford University in 2005–2009, **10 per cent** of couples **met through a colleague** or **at work.** A UK poll in 2013 found that **14 per cent** of couples who met at work **got married**, making the office the top place to find a spouse.

✔ DATING SMART

If you're falling for a colleague, it can be hard to think clearly – you're with them every day. Some important points to consider:

✔ **Does the company have a policy** about employee dating?

✔ **Do either of you handle confidential information** that the other mustn't be privy to?

✔ **Does your profession have harsh penalties** for professional misconduct? If worst came to worst, could you lose your licence?

✔ **How secure are your job positions,** for you and your potential partner?

✔ **How is your standing** with your colleagues?

✔ **How much does your job depend on networking,** popularity, and/or reputation?

✔ **How do you and your potential partner rank** against each other in terms of job titles? If one of you is more senior, could that mess up the chance of an equal relationship?

✔ **How would it affect your working relationship** and your positions in the company if you broke up?

✔ **Is your colleague actually available,** or would dating them interfere with an established relationship?

✔ **Can you see yourself having a serious enough relationship** with this person to make the difficulties worth it?

✔ **In short,** after weighing up all the factors, do you think that dating your colleague is a wise choice?

WOULD LIKE TO MEET...

NAVIGATING THE PERSONAL ADS

Taking out a personal ad in your favourite paper or magazine may be worth trying – after all, you never know who might be reading it – but how do you advertise for love in such a tiny space?

The best thing about a personal ad is that it casts your net into very selective waters. That magazine or paper is read by a specific demographic. Upmarket suburbanites, planet-loving recyclers, pedigree dog-breeders: every periodical caters to a particular market, and that market will include a lot of your sort of person, especially if it reflects your tastes and values.

Fitting into the space

Column inches cost money, and your average personal ad is only a sentence or two. There are positives and negatives to this. On the one hand, it's not very informative: someone may say they have "GSOH" (good sense of humour), but unless you've actually heard their jokes, those four letters tell you pretty much nothing about whether they'll make

you laugh. On the other hand, the task of fitting yourself into a couple of lines tells a reader one important thing: how the person advertising handles a challenge.

It's easy to sound too generic – a good way to stand out is to be honest. Even if you don't fit the "perfect" template we're all held up to, different people like different things and almost everybody likes confidence. If you can present your differences cheerfully – "Short beardy dork seeks love" or "Me: messy hair, big bottom. You: into travel and hiking?" – you'll convey a lot more charm than if you play it safe.

> Divorced dad seeks kind, funny woman for picnics and romance.

Striking a balance

Ads have to say both who you are and what you want. Studies suggest that a good ratio is 7 to 3: that is, 70 per cent about what you're like, so the reader can decide if you sound

appealing, and 30 per cent about what you're looking for.

It's also wise to make your "seeks" positive: a man who "seeks very slim woman", for instance, may find that many slim women will assume he's shallow and pass him by. If a physical type matters that much to you, try to think of it in terms of lifestyle, like "sporty" (muscular) or "food-loving" (not skinny). Be realistic, too: if you aren't exactly a supermodel yourself, you shouldn't expect it of a partner. You can always ask for a picture later.

Anthropology professor Douglas Raybeck describes people's personal ads as "meta-statements about the kind of person they are." In other

2:1

Twice as many men as women describe themselves in personal ads as **"honest"**.

35%

Being discreet, **personal ads** are a sly way to look for **action on the side**: a popular but unsubstantiated statistic is that **35 per cent** of personal ad users are **married**. Whether or not that's an accurate figure, it's worth being aware of the possibility: if your date is **cagey about their home life,** take care.

ACRONYMS AT A GLANCE

BBW / BHM – Big beautiful woman / Big handsome/hunky man

D – Divorced

DTE – Down to earth

HWP – Height and weight proportional

IPT – Is partial to

ISO – In search of

NK – No kids

NS – Non-smoker

NSA – No strings attached

VGL – Very good looking

WLTM – Would like to meet

WTR – Willing to relocate

X – Extreme (usually meaning open to unusual sexual exploits)

420 / 420-FRIENDLY – Pot smoker / doesn't mind if others are

---

words, what someone says in an ad isn't a literal description, but a portrait of their values and personality. Study other ads before you write your own. Which ones would you answer? Learn from the best and get yourself out there!

> Mature lady seeks gentleman escort for elegant nights on the town.

Recording yourself

Some personal ads include the chance to record a voice message on a dedicated line so that suitors can call and listen to it before speaking to you in person. Should you try to sound sexy, or use your normal voice?

It probably depends on your gender. A study by psychology professor Susan Hughes found that men were not very good at making their voices sound more attractive –

in fact, when they tried, they sounded slightly less attractive – while women were able to do so without much difficulty. Exactly what sounds attractive in a female voice can be complicated: studies suggest that men broadly prefer a higher-pitched voice, but women flirt by getting deeper and breathier to signal they're interested. Men were better able to sound more confident, but should probably leave sounding sultry to the ladies.

Whatever your gender, the best advice is probably to try out your message on a friend, then go for it and try not to worry. Everyone is self-conscious about their recording, but the calmer you are, the better – and more attractive – you'll sound.

🔍 WHAT YOU THINK THEY WANT

Heterosexual lonely-hearts tend to word their ads to reflect what convention says the opposite sex desires. A study back in 1977 found that women tended to focus on being pleasing – "outgoing", "sense of humour", "slim", and "attractive" cropped up a lot – while men focused on sounding solvent, using words such as "professional" or "homeowner".

Times may have changed since then, but not entirely: do the ads in your chosen publication still sound that way?

THE FIVE-MINUTE MILE
SPEED DATING

Speed dating – an evening of short meetings with a whole roomful of potential dates, followed by introductions to "matches" who gave each other the thumbs up – is a popular singles activity. Does it work?

It may sound shallow to think you can decide whether you like someone in the few minutes speed dating allows, but in fact the idea was first proposed by Rabbi Yaacov Deyo and his wife Sue Deyo in 1999 with a view to promoting marriage. Reasoning that young people benefited from having elders help them seek out a partner, and aware that the Western world had more or less phased out the traditional matchmaker, the Deyos set up a series of events in Los Angeles, only to have the phenomenon go worldwide.

Can you decide that fast?

Studies of speed dating suggest that we do, in fact, tend to decide whether we're attracted to people pretty fast. Data collected from 10,526 people using an American speed dating service found that looks were the first thing people noticed: religion, income, and personality came into play only if someone had passed on first glance. This was pretty much the same for both men and women.

It's worth remembering, though, that a speed date event is not a neutral environment: when you know you have to decide at once, in a room full of other possibilities, you may jump to conclusions more quickly than you would somewhere calmer and less artificial. The event is explicitly set up on the premise that you should sort through who you fancy and who you don't at speed, without more measured deliberation.

What does this mean for romance?

One lesson we might draw is this: we should be open to the possibility of unexpected compatibilities. A study by American psychologists Sheena

Iyengar and Raymond Fisman presented participants with questionnaires before, just after, a month after, and six months after a speed dating event, asking them to rate out of ten how important certain qualities were:

- attractiveness
- shared interests
- sense of humour
- sincerity
- intelligence
- ambition.

The results were curious: the first, third, and fourth questionnaires were consistent with each other, but if a participant met someone they really liked who didn't fit their "priorities", the second questionnaire – that is, the one they filled in just after meeting this interesting stranger – would change. Now the qualities of the interesting stranger ranked higher: a dater who'd ranked humour low, for instance, would rate it as important if they'd been charmed by someone funny. Long term, though, they didn't change these ideas (now somewhat disproven) about what they valued. In effect, meeting someone unexpectedly attractive reminded these people that their tastes were more diverse than they believed – but then they just forgot again after a while.

⊘ PLEASING THE LADIES?

A study by Stanford University found that certain ways of talking increased a man's chance of being rated well by a female partner. Favourite moves were:

✔ **Being appreciative.** ("That's great!" "Good for you.")

✔ **Sympathizing.** ("That sounds rough.")

✔ **Engaged interrupting** – adding to a thought he agrees with.

✔ **Keeping the questions down.** Women reported that having to answer lots of questions made it hard to keep a conversation going.

✔ **Sharing stories.** This can be entertaining and helps carry the conversation along.

✔ **Varying the tone of your voice to show enthusiasm.** A man who sounds engaged is more exciting.

Are you a man thinking of going on a speed date? Be supportive, share experiences rather than asking questions, and try not to drone.

Worth trying

The implication is that we're capable of liking a broader range of people than we think. Speed dating may or may not introduce us to our future partner – the odds of Mr or Ms Perfect being in any given sample of 25-odd people aren't all that high – but if nothing else, it's a great way to remind ourselves that there are lots of attractive people out there.

If you've been single for a long time, a speed date can be a good way to get back into the swing of flirting and choosing in a safe environment. You may, of course, meet someone wonderful, but even if you don't, try to enjoy yourself and see if the new experience gives your confidence a boost.

In a Stanford study, **women** on speed dates were **more selective than men**, reporting fewer rates of **"clicking"** with a partner.

Usually, **women sit and men rotate** from one partner to the next. In a role reversal at Northwestern University, **men sitting** became the **picky ones** and **women rotating** and making the approach became **less selective**.

The University of Pennsylvania studied a chain of **speed dating events** in 2005 and found that most people **made their decision** within **three seconds** of meeting.

DATING ON THE INTERNET
THE STRANGE WORLD OF INFINITE CHOICE

There's a world of possible partners out there, but sometimes they can be hard to meet. Enter the Internet, the biggest dating scene of them all. Is it all that different from "reality"?

With so much of life online, why wouldn't we use the Internet to meet people? If you live a busy life in a settled social circle, it makes sense: everyone on a dating site is looking for love (or at least for fun), and you can meet people who might never normally cross your path.

A new chance

For those of us who aren't dating our way merrily through college, the vast scale of the Net is a real advantage: studies find that people who have a narrower "market" for partners – such as gay people and middle-aged heterosexuals – are particularly likely to find love online. It's also a boon for shy people: a study published in 2014 in *Computers in Human Behaviour* found that the biggest predictor of choosing online dating was being "rejection-sensitive". Browsing an online profile is a lot less scary than walking up to someone in a bar.

A lot of people who've had bad experiences in the past are moving online: a 2006 American study found that negative experiences with previous relationships tended to correlate with a positive attitude to Internet dating. Of course, this may mean some people on dating sites are thin-skinned or bitter, but it also means there's a dating pool of determined optimists who haven't given up on love.

Managing expectations

Given that all the world seems to be online, it's a good idea to sound a few notes of caution before throwing ourselves into the Net. Dating sites do increase the number of people we can meet, but they don't guarantee a perfect partner; if you're determined to find love, keep your eyes open offline as well as on. The sheer numbers can also send us into a spin. Online relationships tend to be shorter because expectations are

higher: the "shopping list" effect can damage our ability to compromise, leading us to reject quite attractive people in the hope that there's someone better out there, or getting overwhelmed and blaming ourselves if we don't find a "perfect" match. On the other hand, as UK Internet psychologist Graham Jones remarks,

🔍 FEELING TOO OLD TO DATE ONLINE?

Think again. Older daters are taking to the Internet with great success. The main difference between your age group and younger people is that older people tend to be pickier. Especially women – after nurturing kids or a career, for example, if you've finally gained some freedom, why give that up for a less-than-wonderful partner? If someone does seem right, though, older daters are willing to travel further to meet them. As the *International Journal of Aging and Human Development* reports, older Internet daters are eager to meet the right person, but not desperate to meet just anyone.

1 in 3

In the USA in 2013, **one third of marriages** that year were found to have **begun online;** those couples reported slightly **greater satisfaction** than the others and were slightly less likely to divorce.

In 2014, estimates for the **annual revenue** from the **US online dating industry** ranged from **$1.25 billion** to **$2.1 billion.**

$2.1 billion

52%

40 million

In the USA, a country with around 54 million single people, **40 million** have tried **online dating** – whether they're all single is another matter.

30%

30 per cent of **heterosexual couples** in the USA meet online.

61%

61 per cent of **same-sex couples** in the USA meet online.

48%

Numbers are pretty evenly split when it comes to **men and women searching online:** a US estimate in 2014 puts it at **52.4 per cent men, 47.6 per cent women.**

"Because people are seeing more fish in the sea, their final chosen date is much more likely to get more commitment."

In short, online dating sites can be a head-bender, so it's important to stay sane and remember that the aim is to find someone you like rather than prove something about yourself as a person.

On the positive side, there's one great advantage: you know that whoever you see on a dating site definitely is looking to meet someone. That removes the heart-crushing anxiety of wondering whether you're about to hit on someone who turns out to be unavailable. As new media psychologist and researcher Catalina Toma puts it, "Online daters are a self-selected group, who have decided to invest time, energy, effort, and often money (for paid sites) into finding a romantic partner. Therefore, their motivation to build satisfying relationships may be higher."

From building an online profile to meeting a date, handling Internet romance is a definite skill, which we'll discuss in detail over the next few pages. If you do find someone who suits you, though, statistics suggest your relationship will be a good one.

SIGNING UP ONLINE
CREATING A PROFILE

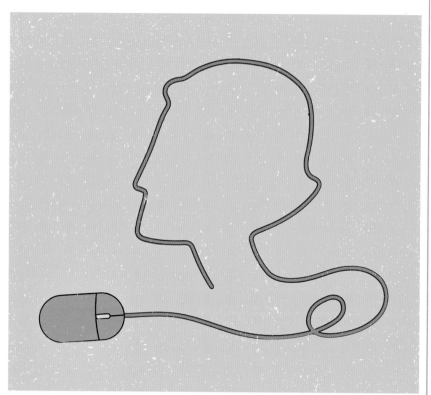

We all want to be loved for ourselves, but with only a photo and a form to fill in, how do we present ourselves to catch the eye? And with so much choice out there, how far can we trust computers as matchmakers?

The number-one rule when it comes to creating a dating site profile is this: you're advertising yourself, and you want to advertise to the right "customers". Dating sites run on algorithms that recommend people to each other based on the data they enter, but as computers can't understand or interpret the information they process, you should see the profile you create for yourself as manipulating the algorithm rather than being at its mercy.

What is an algorithm?

Put simply, an algorithm is a means of solving a mathematical problem through a step-by-step, repeatable process. On dating sites, the "problem" is feeding a computer program a limited amount of information about complex human beings and matching them up with others who might, based on that information, be compatible. The trouble is, we can't feed our everyday behaviour into a questionnaire. The data we're asked for tends to be about our tastes, life, and values. As social psychologist Eli Finkel points out, "The strongest predictors of relationship well-being, such as a couple's interaction style and ability to navigate stressful circumstances, cannot be assessed with such data." Compared with traditional, human matchmakers, computers are a bit short on intuition and common sense – they do exactly what you tell them and no more.

Honest but positive

To beat the algorithms, successful users present an "ideal", but not an inaccurate, version of themselves. Online daters are aware that it's easy to lie on a website, and are usually

HOW TO BREAK IT DOWN

Wondering how to present yourself? An American study of 294 participants (both gay and heterosexual) found you could group your priorities in a partner into three broad categories: physical, personality, and lifestyle. Your photo will take care of the first, so try keeping your profile focused on the other two.

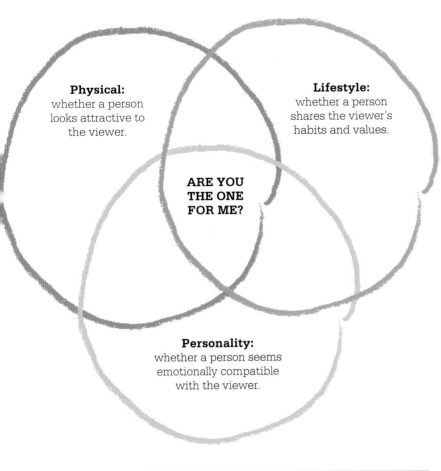

Physical: whether a person looks attractive to the viewer.

Lifestyle: whether a person shares the viewer's habits and values.

ARE YOU THE ONE FOR ME?

Personality: whether a person seems emotionally compatible with the viewer.

TIPS FOR DATING BY NUMBERS

In a popular TED talk, digital strategist Amy Webb describes how she found a partner online by creating a database:

1 **Create a list of the values** you look for in a mate – attitudes to family or faith, aspirations, etc.

2 **Rank these in order of priority,** and give each of them a score based on their importance to you.

3 **Create a scoring system:** for Amy, 700 points meant "Contact"; 900 meant "Go on a date"; 1,500 meant "Consider the possibility of a long-term relationship".

For profiles, Amy found it pays to:

- **Keep the profile short** (100 words average) but well written.

- **Stick to key information** rather than wasting space on superficial "data points" like favourite movies.

- **Use words that sound optimistic and approachable,** such as "fun", "love", "like", and "enjoy".

- **E-mail during daytime hours,** and leave a reasonable amount of time between contacts: about a day (the same sort of time you'd leave between phone calls, for example).

- **Use a flattering photo** – not all-revealing, but attractive and sexy.

disappointed or annoyed if a first date reveals someone who looks and acts nothing like the profile that caught their fancy. Photos need to be recent and information needs to be truthful; after all, you'll quickly get found out if you actually meet up. That said, a profile is not the place to be self-deprecating: people usually browse quickly and if you don't think you're a catch, they may take your word for it and move on. Present your "best self": that's the custom in online dating, and that's what browsing suitors will expect to see.

Online dating offers a dizzying array of options that can be daunting if you're new to the scene, but a positive profile, a flattering photo, and a thick skin can work wonders. Turn over the page for some tips on photos and on picking the right site for you.

»

✓ SO WHAT'S A GOOD PHOTO?

Obviously you want to be wearing flattering clothes and standing somewhere fun (your true love probably won't be ready to see you in your tattered PJs and messy living room just yet), but there are a few good tips to bear in mind.

1 **Keep it real.** The human eye is very good at spotting the difference between a "social smile", where just the mouth muscles are working, and a real smile, which reaches the eyes. If you faked a smile for the photo, people can probably tell, and it risks making you look phony. Use a photo that shows you really enjoying yourself.

2 **Get the eyeballing right.** A straight gaze looks assertive, while gazing down at the camera looks dominant and gazing up looks submissive. Looking slightly at an angle is often the friendliest. Whichever option you choose, it's best to avoid extremes.

Picking a site

Internet dating costs money: a 2014 estimate found that the average US customer spent $239 per year – which is probably less than you'd spend on drinks in cruising bars, but still, no small sum. How much you can afford will likely influence how many sites you sign up on. If you need to be selective, you will probably want to research the companies, as some sites cater to specific demographics and others have specific values that may or may not reflect your own.

A good test is to fill in a dating site's questionnaire: you don't have to post the profile if you decide against the site, but the kinds of questions it asks you will give you strong hints as to what it expects its customers to care about.

Online dating isn't a completely neutral zone – the "halo effect" (see opposite) still holds true when it comes to profile pictures – but remember that an honest but positive profile, an engaging photo, and a thick skin can work wonders.

$239

In the USA, the average **online dating customer** spends **$239 per year** signing onto dating sites.

3 Think body language.

The more space your body occupies, the more confident you look. Likewise, the stiller you are, the more formal you seem, and possibly the more confident (think of a king gazing thoughtfully from his throne). If you're making a gesture, or the wind's blowing your hair, you look lively and playful – that's great as long as it's real. Again, people are good at detecting fakery. (For more on body language, see pages 112–115.)

4 Like your photographer.

Avoid using selfies, which often come out looking either vain or self-conscious. There are lots of studios offering shots – and videos – that look attractive but natural. Talk to the photographer before you commit, to make sure they put you at ease, because that's how you want to look on the site. For a cheaper option, ask a close friend to go somewhere nice with you and snap away. Make the trip as fun and companionable as possible – when there's someone you love behind the camera, you'll give it an affectionate look, and people are more likely to think, "I want that person to look at me like that!"

✎ THE HALO EFFECT STRIKES AGAIN

Attractive people are considered by others to have many positive qualities – remember the "halo effect" on page 44? In a study reported in 2012, 50 women rated 100 dating photos and texts taken from men's profiles on a popular dating site. The results showed that men with attractive photos wrote texts that were rated as more attractive. It seems individuals with attractive profile photos are viewed more favourably overall, but no research has yet established whether they indeed have more positive qualities.

⚠ BEWARE THE SCAMS

Sadly not everyone on a dating site is looking for love, so you need to protect your wallet as well as your heart. Scammers trawl the Net looking for trusting souls to wheedle money out of. If someone seems to send you contradictory information (they're 24 years old, but they've been a doctor for 15 years; they live in a house – no wait, an apartment), be careful. Above all, never send money. They want to visit you but can't afford the ticket? Then why were they courting someone who didn't live anywhere near them? Dating site scammers are horrible people – don't let yourself be taken in.

⚠ SAFE SITES

Not all dating sites are ethical: do read their terms and conditions and check their billing practices before you give them any details. Also, use search engines to check their reputation: sites such as *onlinedatingmagazine.com* and *Ripoff Report* may help you spot which ones you should avoid.

JUST A CLICK AWAY

STARTING A CONVERSATION

So, someone's profile has caught your eye, and you think they might be worth approaching. Or you get a "like" for your profile. How do you go from virtual window-shopping to an actual conversation?

When it comes to meeting someone on a dating site, the transition from admiring their picture to first making contact can be a bit of a leap. Some sites make things easier by having a "like" or a "wink" function, so you can tell the online "matchmaker" that you like the cut of someone's jib and see if they like you back before you put yourself out there. If you're shy, that can be an excellent way to start things, but on other sites you need to send just a short message.

> The whole point is to try and establish that you have things to talk about, so if the other person isn't really talking, there's only so far you can go with that.
>
> **"Christie"**
> Internet dater

Shopping around

The best way to protect yourself psychologically is to regard the dating site as an experimental zone. You don't really know someone from a profile, and they don't know you either. If you put out a feeler and they don't respond, look on it as an experiment that didn't pan out rather than a personal rejection: everyone has idiosyncratic preferences, and you just didn't happen to have or show whatever particular thing they were looking for. Even a brief message is best treated as an act of curiosity rather than hope, since you'll probably have to send quite a lot of them before you hit it off with someone.

How to start talking

If your initial greeting or theirs receives a response, how do you get things going? On most dating sites you make a comment on something in their profile and see if it starts a conversation: savvy Internet daters sometimes even include things in their profile specifically to give suitors the opportunity to mention them.

Verbal chemistry is like physical chemistry: either it happens or it doesn't. If the person looks good on their profile but you can't get talking with them, chances are they'd bore you in real life, so there's no point worrying about them. There are so many people on a dating site that the speed of dismissal in the early stages is very fast: don't take it personally when it happens to you, and don't hesitate to do it when someone doesn't appeal to you.

Brakes off!

Remember this: online, we tend to get more blunt and impulsive. In 2004, US psychologist John Suler described six factors that create the "online disinhibition effect":

I just want casual sex – interested?

TOP THREE MIXED-BLESSING APPROACHES

Everyone is looking for something to say, and original comments stand out. Some approaches may seem like a good idea, but it's worth weighing up the pros and cons.

Approach	Example	Pro	Con
Plain physical compliment	"Hey, looking good, how are you?"	If you and they just want a casual hook-up, this can help cut to the chase.	If you want a proper relationship, it sounds shallow and forward.
Spotting a shared interest	"That's my favourite movie too!"	If you find you have interesting things to say about this, it can be a way of connecting.	A shared taste doesn't mean compatibility: if the conversation doesn't quickly turn into something more than, "Yes, we both like this", it grows dull.
Being "quirky"	"What would you do if you met a walrus?"	This has the advantage of not being crass – and if you're funny, it can turn into a game.	Being deliberately "random" can feel strained, and if it doesn't quickly turn into conversation, it's irritating.

- **Dissociative anonymity.** What you do online doesn't connect to your offline self.

- **Invisibility.** You can't see someone's face when you say something to them, so you don't feel your effect on them.

- **Asynchronicity.** The gap between what you say and when someone hears it makes the Net a somewhere-and-nowhere land.

- **Solipsistic introjection.** When the only person in the conversation actually present is yourself, everyone else's thoughts and feelings are guesswork.

- **Dissociative imagination.** Nothing feels quite real.

- **Minimizing of authority.** No one's in charge, so you can get away with things.

At its most extreme, the effect is well observed in trolls and harassers, but with dating, think of it this way: how someone reacts to having "no rules" tells you something important about them. Sit back and observe with a shrewd eye – and of course, try not to forget your own manners.

It's not always easy if somone upsets you. Internet comments can feel as if they're coming from out of the aether, and if the aether tells you "Ugh, not dating you", that hurts your confidence. Remind yourself that even if you couldn't see their face, it was just one individual – and resolve to save your attention for people who deserve it.

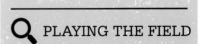

🔍 PLAYING THE FIELD

Trying not to lose it? Think of Internet dating as a game, not as real romance. Child psychologists have long observed that the best way to make something seem safe is to say "This is play". If people can be ruder online because of the not-quite-real quality, you can take advantage of that same unreality to cushion your feelings. You're not laying your heart on the line: you're a detective searching for clues. Matches that don't pan out are red herrings, not painful rejections, so don't be distracted by them for long.

YOU CAN ASSESS COMPATIBILITY BETTER IN 10 MINUTES OF FACE-TO-FACE TIME THAN 100 HOURS OF PROFILE BROWSING

ELI FINKEL, PROFESSOR OF SOCIAL PSYCHOLOGY, NORTHWESTERN UNIVERSITY

CHAPTER 3
DATING
MAKING IT WORK

PICKING A WINNER
THE FIRST DATE

However you meet, once it gets to the first date it's just you, your date, and your expectations. If you are clear about what you're looking for, you stand the best chance of spotting early on who really deserves you.

Unless your first meeting with someone was one of those rare occasions where you had so much to say to each other that a first official date feels more like the continuation of something than the start of it, the first date is a process of mutual experiment. You'll be spending the evening or afternoon with someone you like the look of but don't know very well. It can be a good idea, then, to be sure you understand your own feelings clearly: they're your guide when it comes to deciding whether this date is worth following up.

Are you seeing what's there?
Remember self-verification (pages 32–33), the process by which we tend to seek out people who confirm our self-image, even if that means preferring people who don't actually like us? This concept can be very useful for learning from our past patterns in romance. When it comes to checking out a new date, there's another, complementary concept that's equally useful: "confirmation bias".

Put simply, this is our tendency to be selective when it comes to collecting evidence. While self-verification leads us to choose evidence that confirms our self-image, confirmation bias is broader: we choose to notice things that confirm what we wish to believe. This isn't confined to interpersonal dynamics: politicians favour evidence that supports their agenda; writers and thinkers notice examples of their worldview more readily than counter-examples; psychologists remember the case studies that support their theories better (which is why studies have to have controls). When it comes to dating, too, there's something important to remember: you are going into this date with some very strong wishes.

What do you want?
If you're looking for a committed romantic relationship and you find your date attractive, it can be tempting to ignore signs that they aren't interested in commitment – and to exaggerate hints that they might be. Conversely, if you want to take things slowly and your date is very keen, chances are that your brain will prompt you to shy away from – or selectively overlook –any talk of commitment.

Attraction to someone unsuitable can get us all into trouble on occasion, and confirmation bias is one big reason why. If we want someone, we want to believe things will work out – and we don't always spot any signs to the contrary.

It's important, then, to sort out in your own mind what you hope for in this date. Of course, your hopes may be reasonable – and being excited about someone is an important part of a healthy relationship. You may find you're on surer ground, though, if you can be clear that the promising signs you see when you first meet really are there. Try the exercises opposite to help put your confirmation bias in its place.

CONFIRMATION BIAS

The brain is prone to noticing, retaining, prioritizing, and recollecting information that confirms what it already believes. We think we have evidence to support our opinions, and we do: it's just that we're good at overlooking the evidence against them. This bias can start at any of the levels below, and spread to the others.

Looking only for evidence that confirms our ideas rather than testing them against counterevidence	Taking the evidence that agrees with our ideas more seriously than the evidence that disagrees	Being unconsciously selective in what we call to mind when thinking about past events and relationships
Biased search	**Biased interpretation**	**Biased memory**

✎ WHAT ARE YOU CONFIRMING?

Before you go on your first date, try completing this checklist of what you want. Write down your hopes and put them somewhere safe so you can go over them after the date.

- **I'm the sort of person that attractive people see as...**

- **The kind of relationship I really want is...**

- **The kind of relationship I think I deserve is...**

- **The kind of relationship I'm likely to get is...**

- **I really hope this new person I'm dating will...**

- **I really hope they won't...**

- **What I most want out of this date is...**

Remember, wanting what you want is perfectly reasonable. In fact, it's the only foundation for an authentic relationship. Writing it out will help clarify what you feel, and that can help you separate your hopes from your experiences.

✎ GATHER YOUR DATA!

Immediately after the date – assuming that you and your date haven't ended up in bed or running off to Las Vegas to get married – try completing this second checklist. Do it straight away, while your memory is fresh.

- **What kind of relationship do I think this person wants?**

- **Did they give any signs that they were the kind of person I'm looking for?**

- **Any signs they might not be the kind of person I'm looking for?**

- **Moments when I felt particularly good:**

- **Moments I felt not so good:**

- **Did they say or do anything I wish they hadn't?**

- **What do I think they feel about me?**

If the conclusion is that you don't feel like dating this person again, that settles it – but if you feel like you might, put your answers away and don't look at them for a while.

✎ GOING OUT AGAIN?

Just before going on a second date, fill in the first checklist again, without re-reading your previous notes.

After the second date, fill in the second checklist again.

Next morning, get out all four lists, compare your answers, and ask yourself:

1 **Is there anything I tried to ignore** from the first date to the second one?

2 **Does my image of myself** before the second date sound better or worse than before the first?

3 **Is the impression this person** is giving me consistent?

If you decide to date this person again, consider doing these exercises for as long as you find them helpful.

To deserve you, your date should inspire answers that trend in a positive direction: their intentions should be clear, harmonious with yours, and unmarred by events you're trying to ignore. Then you'll be confident that your confirmation of their hopes comes from their behaviour, which means your hopes have a good chance of being met.

LOOKING THE PART

HOW TO PUT YOUR BEST FACE FORWARD

It's the big night and you want to make a good first impression. How do you present yourself to look as comfortable and desirable as possible, while still feeling like your real self?

✓ SUIT YOURSELF

- Get clothes that fit you nicely. Dress for the size you are, not the size you wish you were: no one will see the label but you, and every figure looks best when the clothes hang right. Besides, you're meeting someone who was willing to go out with you based on how you look now, so clearly they like it. Embrace it.

- Find colours that complement your skin tone. If you aren't sure what's right for you, grab your artiest or best-dressed friend and ask them to give you some quick tips.

- Don't wear anything uncomfortable, no matter how good it looks. Surreptitious squirming or scratching won't show you at your best.

✓ SUIT THE SETTING

- Be clear in advance where you're going, and pick something appropriate to wear. A first date in a gallery and a first date on a stroll in the park need different outfits.

- Be prepared for weather changes, especially if you live in an unpredictable climate. Shivering or sweating doesn't look very elegant, and the last thing you want is to end up cutting a lovely evening short because you just can't stand the temperature any more.

- Wear comfortable shoes. That doesn't mean they have to be hiking boots, but successful dates can last an unexpectedly long time and you may find yourselves walking around looking for new places to hang out. Walking is easier than limping.

PUTTING A GOOD FACE ON IT

- Make-up or not? Shave or stubble? Your best bet is probably to do a nice version of your usual self. You're showing your date an image of a person they might have a relationship with, not posing for a photoshoot: don't commit to a look you don't want to maintain.

- Gentlemen: are you hoping for a kiss? Be aware that stubble burn can be something of a damper. If your five o'clock shadow is part of your rugged charm, by all means keep it, but consider softening it with some conditioner before you go out – and if you do get to smooch your date, be a bit gentle about it. Some people's skin is more sensitive than others', and you don't want to be remembered as "that guy with the sandpaper face".

- Wear glasses? Wear them on the date. You need to have a pair that suits you, but if they do, there's no reason to pretend: as long as they're flattering and well-maintained, glasses are fine. If this becomes a relationship, your date is going to see a lot more of them, so you might as well start as you mean to go on.

- Choosing a perfume or aftershave? Use it lightly: your natural smell can contain pheromones you don't want to smother. (See pages 48–49 for more about the scent of attraction.)

- Brush your teeth and don't eat anything too lingering. Man or woman, no one wants to kiss a smelly date: it's not only unpleasant, but also implies that you're inconsiderate about the other person's comfort.

 SUIT YOUR MOOD

- Want to strike a particular note? A study in 2002 found that clothing affects our style of speech: formally dressed people used more formal adjectives to describe themselves than the casually dressed, who described themselves in more colloquial terms. Both groups also responded faster to the type of adjectives used by other people that matched their style of dress.

- If you've got a favourite outfit that suits the setting, it'll make you feel your natural self, which is what you want your date to fall in love with.

- Choose a style that reflects your personality. Flashy and fabulous or discreetly classic, dress as the person you hope the relationship will allow you to be, and see if your date thinks you look wonderful.

⊗ SHADES OF PERFECTION?

Is there a perfect colour to wear on a date? Consider these examples of the kind of recommendations you see in a lot of magazines and articles online:

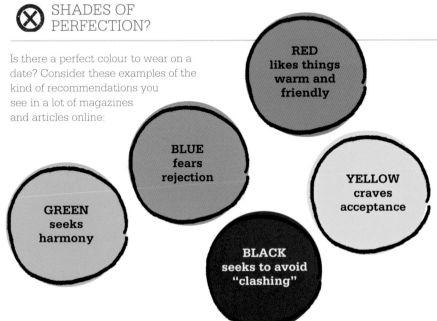

RED
likes things
warm and
friendly

BLUE
fears
rejection

GREEN
seeks
harmony

YELLOW
craves
acceptance

BLACK
seeks to avoid
"clashing"

Convinced? Because the thing is, we made up those descriptions with a single purpose in mind: they all mean the same thing and they could apply to just about anybody. Everyone would rather be warmly accepted than rejected! If you get advice like that you're probably looking at the Forer effect (see pages 52–53). People aren't computers and we can't key in colour codes to get a desired response.

As a general rule, ignore the pop-psychology advice and go with whatever looks best on you. If your date likes you, it will take more than the colour of your coat to put them off.

IT'S GOING TO BE FINE

CONFIDENCE-BUILDING EXERCISES

Dressed and pressed, but still not feeling quite ready to go out the door and meet your new date? Then try some confidence-building exercises to help ease your anxiety and put you in a better frame of mind.

When we get anxious, it hits us in the amygdala – the part of the brain that registers fear, and which gives us a racing heart, sweaty palms, and even shaky legs. The increased heart rate and shaky limbs are the body preparing to make a run for it, and the sweat is to help us cool down while we fight or flee – but you might want to try some more productive methods of handling the nerves...

PITCH OR POCKET?

Worried whether you'll make a good impression?

What to do: Write down reasons you do and don't feel confident. Bin the "don'ts" but keep the "do's". A series of studies in Spain found that treating thoughts as if they were physical objects could be effective: volunteers wrote down what they liked or disliked about their bodies, and then kept the page or ripped it up and tossed it. Throwing the "don'ts" away made them feel better than keeping them.

Tip: Physically throwing or storing the paper helps more than just imagining it, so go through the actual motions.

WRITE IT UP

How will I cope if this date doesn't go well?

What to do: Write a list of everything good, smart, kind, interesting, and cool you've done in the past week.

Tip: Do it longhand so you have plenty of time to note the great things you've done. Let yourself see how much there is in your life: you'd be a catch for the right person, and even single you've got a lot going for you.

FIX YOUR POSTURE

On your way to meet your date?

What to do: Sit up. A study at Ohio State University asked people to write down three qualities – either positive or negative – that would affect their future performance in a professional role. They were then asked to either sit up straight or slump forwards, and assess what they'd written down. The sitters-up were much more likely to agree they had the good qualities they'd identified; the slumpers were more likely to dismiss their good qualities as unconvincing, and to believe the bad ones.

Tip: Our bodies assume a pose in line with our emotions – and sometimes emotions in line with our pose. Find the most confident pose you can, and your emotions may follow.

 KEEP SMILING

Feeling shy and miserable?

What to do: Literally, put on a happy face. Research shows our moods tend to follow our expressions, and smiling can make us actually feel happier: psychology calls this the "facial feedback hypothesis". Back in 1988, volunteers who were watching cartoons while holding a pencil horizontally between their teeth – which forced their face into a "smile" by purely physical means – rated the cartoons as funnier than the volunteers who held the pencil between closed lips, which forced their facial muscles into a frown.

Tip: Don't practise smiling in front of a mirror, as this redirects your attention to your eyes rather than your face muscles. Just smile and feel the effects.

 SETTLE YOUR FACE

Feeling a bit frantic?

What to do: Soothe yourself as you would soothe an agitated child: raise a gentle hand to your face and stroke your cheek or forehead. Giving yourself calming stimulation like this is known as "self-soothing", and it's a useful skill for managing emotions.

Tip: While doing this exercise, touch your face as if it were truly precious: you need to remember that it is.

WORK IT OUT

Too much stress to handle?

What to do: Get your body working. Exercise releases endorphins, the stress-busting hormones that block the feeling of pain and create a sense of euphoria, helping you coast over your nerves. It also improves your "fluid intelligence" – that is, intelligence that doesn't require previous knowledge but lets you reason quickly to deal with complex information and form an opinion – just the thing when meeting someone new. It's fine if you're no athlete, as you don't have to run a marathon: anything that gets your heart rate up and helps you break a sweat will do, whether it's a workout at the gym or dancing around singing into your hairbrush. (If you have any medical conditions, check with your doctor about what's safest for you.)

Tip: Bear in mind that exercise raises body temperature and you can keep sweating for a while after you've finished, so it's probably best to do it several hours before the date rather than just before. Get your heart racing with physical activity, and it will settle down to a manageable rate afterwards.

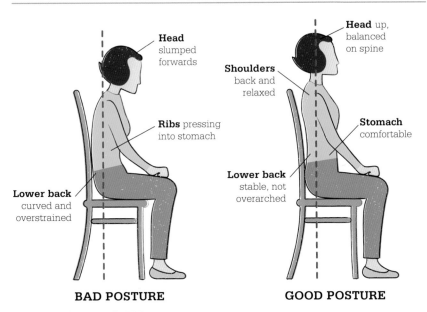

Head slumped forwards

Ribs pressing into stomach

Lower back curved and overstrained

BAD POSTURE

Head up, balanced on spine

Shoulders back and relaxed

Stomach comfortable

Lower back stable, not overarched

GOOD POSTURE

SIT UP STRAIGHT

We've probably all had tiresome teachers criticize our posture, but they may have had a point. A comfortably upright position puts a lot less stress on the body, which means we aren't dealing with physical tension feeding into our mental state – always an advantage when dating.

STRESS-FREE FIRST DATES

WHERE'S THE BEST PLACE TO START?

Of course there's no such thing as a truly stress-free first date – it wouldn't be natural if you weren't a bit keyed up – but choosing a good setting can make things a lot more rewarding.

 THE GREAT OUTDOORS

Getting out into nature is great for feeling like ourselves. A Swedish study in 2010 placed 18 stressed or burned-out volunteers either in an outdoor location or in an indoor simulation of a natural environment. Subjects who got to experience real nature felt a renewed sense of wellbeing and heightened sensory perception, while the people in the artificial environment did not feel any of those benefits.

A stroll outdoors makes for a low-stress first date because it doesn't cost you any money, and nature adds some increased sensory perception and pleasure. It's probably best, though, not to go into the wilderness with someone you've only just met: meeting in public is safer, so see if there's a nice park within reach.

 WHERE TO EAT?

Choosing a restaurant setting to get to know your date? Pick one that plays classical music. In 2001 music therapist Kaja Jensen asked 85 young adults to write or talk about the most significant event of their lives: the ones who did so with classical music playing in the background were more thoughtful and expressive, and reported that they enjoyed the music as well.

Classical isn't everyone's taste, of course, but if you like the idea of an elegant setting where you can open up to each other, a bit of Mozart or Mendelssohn over the speakers might nudge the conversation to a deeper level.

 IT'S ALL IN THE LYRICS

Are you and your date into pop rather than classical? If you're putting on some mood music, go sexy: in 2007, an American study found that volunteers exposed to slightly racy songs gave online profiles higher attractiveness ratings than those who'd been listening to family friendly ones. Avoid degrading or disrespectful lyrics, but a hint of naughtiness over the speakers might help create a spark.

If some live music in a relaxed setting is more your thing, see if there's a local event, fair, or festival that day. Spotting a one-off chance to enjoy something shows you as enterprising and open-minded, and it can be bonding to be in a situation that's new to you both.

 CULTURE VULTURE?

Check out the museums and galleries in your local area. Lots of them are free or reasonably priced, which is helpful for reducing the pressure (and might even help you eliminate a gold-digger: anyone who objects to being taken somewhere cheap and nice is not worth a second date. More importantly, they're an environment where you can walk freely, find plenty of things to talk about, and check out your date's manners when it comes to making space for other patrons, especially if it's crowded.

Even if the date isn't much company, you can still enjoy the culture; if it goes well, though, you may find yourselves with a hundred things to talk about.

 GOOD OLD COFFEE

Meeting for coffee is a classic. It's low investment – a consideration if, for instance, you're dating online and having a lot of meet-ups. And it reduces the pressure to like each other just to get your money's worth.

🔍 STUCK WITH THE STRESS?

We can't magic away anxiety, but we can use it. American and Canadian research in 2009 found that people who were told that nerves improve performance actually did perform better on tests. Tell yourself that your butterflies will help, and they probably will.

✓ DO I HOLD THE DOOR?

Modern men sometimes worry about door etiquette: does holding a door look anti-feminist, or does not holding it look rude? People have different preferences, of course, but here are the default rules:

1 **If you get there first,** hold the door open. It's polite, not excessive; no reasonable woman will object.

2 **If she gets there first,** wait to see what she does. If she's waiting for you to open it, open it; if she makes a move to open it, let her.

3 **If she holds the door for you,** accept her courtesy – insisting she goes first makes things awkward. Go through and say, "Thank you"; that's all you need to be a gent.

4 **If you hold the door for her** and she says, "Thanks", say something appreciative but gender-neutral like "You're welcome" or "My pleasure".

5 **Whatever happens,** don't make a big production of it. Most women don't really mind who opens the door but probably don't want to get into a discussion of traditional gender roles on a first date.

For most people these days, holding the door is less about gender than manners. Treat your date the same way you'd treat anyone you respected, male or female. And don't worry too much: as long as you don't let the door hit her in the face, most women aren't nearly as bothered about this issue as men are.

✗ SOME BAD IDEAS

Certain choices are just not great for a first date. Steer away from:

1 **Home cooking.** Being in the home of a near-stranger is risky and makes many people nervous.

2 **The movies.** Yes, it's a classic, but you won't be able to talk.

3 **Five-star restaurants.** Higher prices, higher pressure.

4 **A nightclub.** You won't be able to hear each other talk.

5 **Your hobby spot.** A date may feel they're just tagging along.

6 **Around friends or family.** Unless your culture calls for chaperones, make it about just the two of you, on neutral ground.

EVERYONE LOVES A GOOD LISTENER

THE ART OF ACTIVE COMMUNICATION

Few things are so beguiling as being at the absolute centre of someone's attention. Since nothing shows attention like good listening, how can we improve our listening skills and bewitch an attractive date?

Most people spend roughly 90 per cent of their waking hours communicating, be it speaking, writing, or listening. Even so, studies show that during that time, we take in only 25 to 50 per cent of what we hear. The rest of the time, we're thinking of how to reply, how we feel about the speaker, or something else entirely. Much as we like to feel in contact with other people, we're less inclined to follow their words closely than to scan them to get the gist of what they're saying.

When it comes to checking out a date, though, the details of what they say are important. Not only do those details give us plenty of clues about the date's attitudes, expectations, and mental habits, but it's also the case that giving someone our full attention is a very good way of gaining theirs. We're social creatures, on the whole, and we tend to be interested in people who treat us like we're interesting. This is where a technique called "active listening" comes in.

🔍 MIRROR NEURONS

The brain possesses certain neurons that help us imitate what we see others do. Known as "mirror neurons", they fire up in response to emotions signalled by other people, making us produce a mirror image of their happiness, distress, or even just their physical actions, like smiles or frowns. As we watch people, we naturally "feel with" them – and the closer we watch, the more connections we make.

ACTIVE LISTENING

The idea of active listening is this: you focus on the person you're speaking to, and use verbal and non-verbal hints both to show them you're paying attention and to keep your attention where it needs to be. Some basic tips:

1 **Keep your mind directed towards the speaker.** Ignore outside distractions as much as you can. Don't get too drawn into internal distractions either, such as what you're going to say in reply or who they remind you of when they say this or that. Focus your attention on the words they say.

2 **Be accepting and empathic.** You may or may not agree with what they're saying, but you can decide that when they've finished. As long as you're listening, see them as an interesting person who has a right to be separate and different from you and whose thoughts and feelings are as vivid and meaningful to them as yours are to you.

3 **Don't jump to speak.** Sometimes a pause is the beginning of an awkward silence, but sometimes the speaker is just gathering their thoughts or stopping for breath. Be sure they're finished before you start talking yourself.

4 **Ask constructive questions.** In particular, encourage the speaker to be specific. If they say their job is exciting, for example, you might ask them what it is that they find exciting: the more detail you have, the more you can picture someone else's experience. (Try not to overdo it, though; being interrupted by a barrage of questions can be off-putting, and makes keeping the conversation going feel like hard work.)

5 **Respond sensitively.** Use language that shows you're listening, such as repeating back what they say or checking what they mean.

6 **Use open body language.** This can include:

Eye contact. Don't stare, of course, because that's uncomfortable and can feel aggressive, but make sure you meet their gaze regularly.

Good facial expressions. Most of us naturally "mirror" the feelings in the face opposite us: let your face show that you're following this person emotionally.

Arms down. Crossed arms makes you look closed off.

Match their stance. When we have a rapport with someone, we often assume a similar posture to theirs: try it and see if it helps.

Appropriate body space. Some people like you to lean closer while they confide, but other people like to keep their distance. Watch for their personal preference. (For more on body space, see page 115.)

The purpose of active listening is not to sit passively and just be talked at, but to be actively engaged while the speaker – in this case, the date you're trying to get to know – tries to communicate what's really on their mind. When you are actively engaged, you and the other person are likely to feel connected, and you'll be experienced by the other person – your date – as someone who is supportive.

> Giving someone our full attention is a very good way of gaining theirs.

🔍 PROSOCIAL GENES

A 2011 study in Toronto found that people born with a particular gene variation tended to use more smiles, nods, and eye contact – what psychologists call "affiliative cues". Couples displaying these were rated as more empathic by strangers who'd watched them on just 20 seconds of soundless video. You may or may not have the gene – called rs53576, it acts on the oxytocin receptors that help us bond – but there's nothing to stop you nodding and smiling: it clearly makes a good impression.

250,000

American anthropologist Ray Birdwhistell estimated that the **human face** is capable of more than a **quarter of a million expressions.** Keep watching for them: it shouldn't get dull!

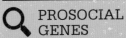

SHRINKING VIOLETS
COPING WITH SHYNESS

If you feel like the anxiety is just too much and you'll never pluck up the courage to approach someone, don't despair – shyness is a lot more manageable than you might think.

One of the most encouraging statistics in psychology comes from Bernardo Carducci of the Shyness Research Institute at Indiana University Southeast: almost half of us consider ourselves to be shy. Mostly we manage to put on a functional public face and relate to others perfectly well. Carducci's statistic tells us one thing above all: the relationship between feeling shy and appearing inadequate is practically nonexistent.

40-45%

Between 40 and 45 per cent of adult **Americans** consider themselves to be **shy.**

What type of shyness is it?
The Shyness Research Institute defines three categories of shyness: cognitive, affective, and behavioural. Put more simply, we can be defeated by our thoughts, our feelings, or our behaviour. Cognitive shyness takes the form of excessive self-criticism or anticipating the worst (see pages 24–25): you tell yourself you're hopeless until you start to believe it. Affective shyness involves feelings of stress and anxiety. Behavioural shyness is what you do – or rather, what you don't do, such as talking to people or going to parties.

The three types of shyness feed on one another. If you think panicky thoughts, then you're likely to have panicky feelings, and vice versa, and you can get into a vicious circle of avoiding contact with people, feeling bad about that, thinking it means you're a failure, and carrying on avoiding everyone. If shyness is getting in the way of you meeting new people, try to observe yourself

ON THE BRIGHT SIDE

Neurologically speaking, shyness may be a sign of deeper thinking. Around 20 per cent of people are born with "sensory perception sensitivity": they are slow to "warm up" as children, are more conscientious, more bored with small talk, and more easily tired by crowds. Such people are prone to shyness, but because their brains process input more actively, they are also more likely to be original and clever.

over the next few weeks and see if you can identify where you think it's most deep-rooted. The more you understand where it's coming from, the better placed you are to tackle it.

How to fix it
The solutions depend on where the root of your shyness lies. If you're starting with negative thoughts, work on some self-affirmation: you're almost certainly more interesting, appealing, and worthwhile than you're telling yourself right now. Get into the habit of spotting and

SHY, OR JUST INTROVERTED?

Many of us are naturally introverted, find social situations tiring, assume there's something wrong with us, and define ourselves as shy. To find out which you are, ask yourself:

When I avoid a social situation, is it because I:
A Can't be bothered tonight; it'll be more fun to stay home?
B Dread it and think I'll be miserable?

At a party, I'm sitting by myself in a quiet corner. Am I:
A Taking time out to recharge my batteries?
B Hiding or wishing I could find someone to talk to?

I'm introduced to a stranger and have to talk to them. Do I think:
A This is going to be a bit of an effort.
B This person will think I'm an idiot.

Mostly A: If you're saying "A", that's introversion and shouldn't worry you – see pages 36–37.
Mostly B: if you're saying "B", that's shyness. Or you could be a bit of both – there is a degree of overlap. Either way, see below for ways to overcome it.

MAKING IT WORSE

Thoughts, feelings, and behaviour can all get into a cycle where each reinforces the other. When it comes to shyness, the key is to figure out which is the starting point and stop it before it all starts to spin out of control.

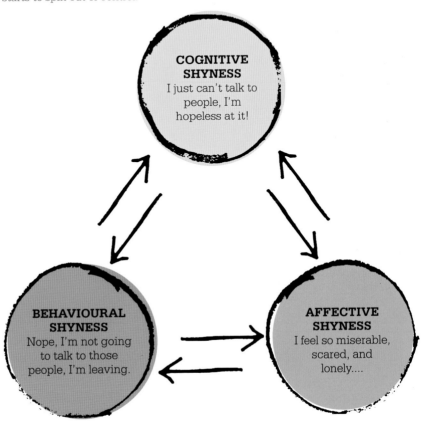

stopping negative thoughts before they get too tight a grip on you: try the exercises on pages 32 and 35.

If you're starting with anxious emotions, self-calming is the way to go. Before you go into stressful situations, try some meditation or self-comforting exercises: see pages 56–57 and 102–103.

With behavioural shyness, the solution is practice. Hard as it may sound, you need to get out into the situations that you fear, and keep going into them: talk to people, even if it's just a few words at the check-

out till. If you have opinions you struggle to express, rehearse them at home so you can say them more confidently in company. Manners, too, can go a long way: if you don't have much to say but you say it politely (throwing in "please", "thank you", and "excuse me"), that's going to please people.

Keep testing yourself in public and reassuring yourself in private, and you'll do just fine.

GOT NOTHING TO SAY?

A lot of us feel shy because we have no faith in our ability to interest or entertain people. The good news is that even if you think you don't have much to say, most people are comfortable with a quiet person as long as they offer a sympathetic ear. If you don't feel you sparkle in conversation, see pages 106–107 to work on your listening skills.

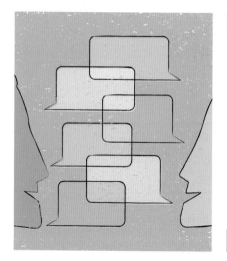

TALKING THE TALK
GETTING A GOOD CONVERSATION GOING

The first few dates are all about establishing a connection, and to do that, you have to talk to each other. If you tend to struggle for words, you may want to polish your conversational skills.

You're such a great listener

First tip: if you get tongue-tied, it's not the end of the world. Most people love to talk about themselves. If you can't think of much to say, focus on asking some open-ended questions and then sitting back to listen: either you'll find yourself relaxing and think of some comments to make, or else you can keep prompting them to talk and be appreciated for your attentiveness – good listening skills are very attractive.

Some useful phrases to help get someone talking:
- What do you think about X?
- What's it like to do X?
- So you like X; what do you like about it?
- So you don't like X; what would you change about it?
- How did you get interested in or start doing X?
- It sounds interesting – can you tell me a bit more?

The key is to ask questions that can't be answered with a simple yes or no: the more open-ended they are, the more expansive your date can be. Just remember to smile, nod, say supportive things, and act interested so they feel heard, not interviewed.

This works best when you follow your own curiosity, so you truly are interested. If it feels like a technique, then consider whether you just need more practice or whether this person really isn't of interest to you.

You're so interesting

Sometimes you meet someone cool who's done all sorts of amazing things that you haven't. They seem so impressive, you hardly know what to say. Maybe you should just give up because you've got nothing to offer.

Not at all. Many people are happy to talk to someone who can admit to being uninformed: after all, they too must have been a novice at some point. They may get irritated if someone pretends to knowledge they don't have, but if you own up to your ignorance confidently, that's fine. They may even find it refreshing: if they're fed up with opinionated bores telling them their business, someone who respects their expertise can be a pleasant change.

That sounds amazing, I'd love to hear about it.

Wow, I don't know anything about that – could you tell me more?

TELL ME MORE
Rather than feeling too intimidated by someone's expertise to join in, try one of these phrases.

Put it this way: their knowing and doing cool things doesn't diminish you, and you get to enjoy it. If you can show honest appreciation, you'll come across as smart, open, and likeable: even the most accomplished person wants a supportive partner. (And if they react to your questions negatively, you probably won't want a relationship with them anyway: would you treat someone like that?)

Now it's your turn

At some point you're going to have to talk about yourself, which means striking a balance between sounding confident and arrogant, modest and hopeless. A few tips:

- **Be enthusiastic** about the things that are important to you. A smart dater is on the lookout for people who can get excited about stuff they love – it means you can get excited about a person you love, too. They don't have to share your tastes to appreciate the joy you take in them: joy itself is attractive.
- **Got some dreams?** Talk about them as things you hope to do rather than things you'll probably never achieve. Be positive and can-do. That's much more appealing, and you may even talk yourself into taking that trip or learning that skill you've always thought about.

 THE NO-NO'S

A first date is really not the time to mention:

- What a rotten person your ex was.
- How annoying you find your family.
- How lonely you've been.
- Your doubts about your worth as a person.

First dates should leave both people feeling hopeful for the future, so stay positive and save the complaints for later.

- **Not so happy** with certain things in your life? You can say so – as long as you don't act like you expect a relationship to fix everything, or like you'd drag someone down. Find counterbalances: yes, your job is dull, but you get a lot out of your social life; true, your place is a bit of a shoebox, but at least that gets you out and about. Treat the drawbacks as incidental rather than the key to your identity. You'll feel happier and more satisfied with life if you can honestly see things with this kind of balance.

 WHICH OF THESE SOUNDS LIKE YOU?

Your date says something that reminds you of a great anecdote from your past? Tell it now! People who can talk interestingly about their experiences are great company. For the best results:

1 **Keep it fairly short** – no more than a minute or so – to avoid dominating the conversation too much. If it's a long story, take breaks to give your date a chance to get a few words in.

2 **Regularly check your date's body language** and expression. If they're leaning away or looking glazed, cut your story short; if they're leaning forward and listening eagerly, you're doing well.

3 **If it's a funny story,** whether or not they laugh is a great indicator of whether you're compatible. (See also pages 50–51.)

4 **Don't be afraid to throw yourself into the performance.** You evidently think this story is worth telling, so do it justice.

5 **A thought to consider privately:** what's the "moral" of this story? What are you telling your date about your worldview? (That people can be surprisingly shrewd? That you can laugh at yourself? That beauty can be found in unexpected places?) Think of what the story means to you, and then see if it means the same thing to your date.

I'd love to know more if you don't mind explaining to a total newbie.

That's really impressive. I've never heard that before – I'd love to know more.

YOU DON'T HAVE TO SAY ANYTHING

BODY LANGUAGE TIPS

Understanding people's body language is key to romantic success, but many of us are not so confident in our abilities. If you're feeling uncertain, what should you do about it?

How do you know whether a date is warm or aggressive, interested or bored, evasive or just nervous? Until the day we have mind-reading technology, we'll have to stick to reading people's bodies.

How are your skills?

You probably already know more about body language than you think – as with every skill, though, some people have more facility than others. For the lucky ones, picking up mood from body language comes naturally: they register the subtle messages of face and gesture so quickly that they reach a conclusion before they notice they're doing it. At the other end of the scale, some of us find body language extremely difficult to understand: we're just born with less "reading" abilities than others; or shyness leads us to avoid other people, so we haven't had the same opportunity to practise.

If you happen not to be one of the body-language maestros, don't worry, there are several good ways to tackle the issue, which are probably best used in conjunction.

Practise, practise, practise

First, to improve your body language reading skills, don't wait till you're on

55%

Studies suggest that **before a man speaks**, his **posture** accounts for up to **55 per cent** of a **woman's first impression** of him.

🔍 LOOKING TO SPOT A LIAR?

US psychologist and body-language expert Paul Ekman claims that the key is to watch for "micro-expressions" – expressions on the face that last about 1/25th of a second. It's hard: he tested 15,000 people and found that most of them needed a 32-hour course before they got the hang of it. Even if we do spot the fact that someone's hiding something, it doesn't mean we know what they're hiding or why. A man who looks awkward when he insists he's single might be lying ... or just embarrassed.

a date. Watch the people around you. Don't gawp, obviously, but if you see someone happy, angry, anxious, or excited, make a mental note of their expression and body language. We learn by watching, and the more you watch, the more you'll absorb.

Between dates is also a good time to practise reading your friends' body language. Start with someone close who knows you well and won't be put out if you check to see whether you've judged their feelings right. It's quite natural to ask: "You seem in a particularly good mood – what's going on?" or "What's up? You seem a bit down today." Or, if you're really unsure of what they're feeling, you can just ask, "How do you feel about what Jamie did?" These are all good questions to ask, even as you get better at reading body language.

Own up

No one wants to be seen as insensitive, but the essence of insensitivity isn't being a bit hopeless at reading people's signals – it's not caring about the feelings those

❓ GETTING YOUR ATTENTION

1 **The attention phase.** In the first of five stages of "love signals" described by the Center for Non-verbal Studies, we signal:

- our gender, acting extra "masculine" or "feminine"

- our presence, making subtle movements to draw the eye, such as walking around or gesticulating more than usual

- our good intentions, by smiling, shrugging, and using open-palm gestures to show we mean no harm.

2 **Looking for a response.** After seeking someone's attention, we see if it's worked. We watch for:

- smiles

- eye contact

- body posture aligned with or mirroring our own

- nervous self-touching (do they want us to touch them?)

- friendly shrugs.

3 **The conversation phase.** If we make a connection, we start to create our own space, and explore:

- sitting face to face and/or intensely focused on each other, making it clear third parties shouldn't join us

- eating together – a universal ritual of bonding and relaxation

- beginning to ask probing questions

- laughing and joking.

4 **The touching phase.** We begin discreetly, and take it from there:

- "accidental" brushes, to see if our date responds, freezes, or flinches

- "intention cues", adopting a posture that shows we'd like to touch, such as extending open arms

- hugging and kissing – a big threshold to greater intimacy.

5 **The love-making stage.** This includes full-on caressing, kissing, and cuddling, as well as sex – the point where we really let our bodies do the talking.

signals indicate. If body language is a real stumbling block for you, it's probably best to be direct with your date. "I'm not that good at reading body language, so if I do anything that bothers you, please just let me know so I can stop!" is a declaration of positive intentions that many people – including the kind of person who'd be right for you – will find sincere and charming. You're showing your good heart there and then. In the meantime, for some more practical tips on body language, see over the page.

🔍 A UNIVERSAL LANGUAGE?

While the basic non-verbal expressions such as smiling and shock are universal (see page 43), be aware of cultural differences: every nation has its own gestures. The United States, for example, is estimated to have about 80 distinct gestures: Americans usually can't name them all, but they can use and recognize them.

»

Getting your own body language right

Communication is a complex business: experts estimate that anything from 60 per cent to 93 per cent of it is non-verbal! If you're anxious about the impression you're making on a date, the tips offered here will help you to ensure that your worries don't show in your body language.

Go with your feelings

Body language is far too complex to learn from a book, but the good news is that you probably already know more about it than you realize. We often pick up signals unconsciously but accurately: a 2014 study at the MIT Media Lab in Cambridge, Massachussetts, found that volunteers distrusted a humanoid robot programmed to give off non-verbal "mistrustful" cues (such as crossing its arms and touching its own face), even though they couldn't necessarily say why.

You don't need to learn body language like a foreign tongue: your emotions will almost certainly be feeding into your body language automatically, and your date will almost certainly be picking up on them. Just work on feeling happy and confident, and you'll more than likely look fine.

GREAT POSTURE

Stance is a clue to confidence: someone standing up straight looks assured and assertive, while someone sagging looks downcast. You should probably avoid extremes: a ramrod-straight back can look tense, more like a soldier getting bawled out by a drill sergeant than like a free adult on a date with someone nice; on the other hand, a deep slump looks both dejected and unhealthy. The Alexander Technique for improved posture recommends that you imagine there's a buoyant balloon in your head, which encourages you to "float" into a naturally upright position.

✔ **Stand tall and confident,** but don't stiffen up: the message you want to convey is "I'm comfortable in my body".

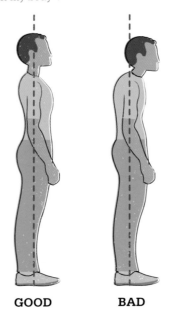

GOOD   **BAD**

STAND EASY

A good natural stance involves the head slightly dropped (so that the neck isn't cramped), shoulders open, tummy in, and back relaxed.

LEARN FROM THE ANXIETY PROS

We all know that fidgeting – shifting around, playing with napkins, tapping our fingers – isn't a good idea on a date, but it can be hard to control. There's a good reason for that: our bodies are giving us anxiety signals, and seeking out sensory input (the feeling of motion or fiddling) helps to override them, in the same way that squeezing a bruised finger can override the pain.

Self-soothing exercises can help (see pages 102–103), but if you really struggle to stay still, take a tip from the experts – people with sensory processing disorders such as ADHD and autism, whose baseline anxiety levels tend to be high. They often keep something squashy, twisty, or highly textured in the pocket: you can play with it out of sight and get some stimulation without looking restless.

✔ **Search online for "fidget toy" or "sensory toy"** – toy shops, too, sell inexpensive little trinkets that can work very well.

✔ **Consider a ring** with a textured band if you're planning to wear a pocketless outfit; you can touch the band with your thumb behind your palm and it won't attract attention.

TWITCHY LEGS?

When we're nervous, a lot of us tap our feet or jiggle our legs – which often distracts and slightly irritates those around us. If you find yourself doing it, crossing your ankles is a good way to regain your poise. Or arrange the date so it includes something active, like going for a stroll, to ease the anxiety.

LOOKING FRIENDLY

Happy to see someone? It will show in your stance. The "welcome" body language crosses cultures, even among blind people who've never seen it. If you're delighted to see your date, you'll probably do the following spontaneously:

- **Raised eyebrows:** the upward-flicking "greeting" expression.

- **Relaxed facial muscles:** no worries, so no grimaces.

- **Open torso,** with loose arms held open or just easy and mobile.

Check your expressions and gestures when you meet your date. If you feel your face tensing up or your arms drawing in, you're probably nervous: take a deep breath, relax, and open up your stance – it will look a lot more welcoming, and feel more relaxed.

THE DUCHENNE SMILE

Smiling is crucial to social relationships: it's the top facial gesture our brains recognize after eye contact. What's the difference between a real smile and a fake one? A real one creases up the skin around our eyes. (So don't worry about crow's feet: they make you look genuine.) Guillaume Duchenne, a 19th-century French neurologist, first identified the difference: a "Duchenne smile" is an authentic one, warm and infectious, while a fake one tends to make people uncomfortable without being sure why.

- ✔ **Smile with both sides of your mouth** – a lopsided smile can be misread as disdainful.

- ✔ **To create your own Duchenne smile,** think happy thoughts; to spot one in your date, see if they're smiling with their eyes.

HANDS UP!

Hand gestures are a huge part of communication: behavioural investigator Vanessa Van Edwards calls them the true "windows of the soul". Hiding your hands looks unconfident: let them move around.

WATCH YOUR PERSONAL SPACE

Anthropologist Edward T. Hall identified four physical comfort zones. Only lovers or close friends can be at an intimate distance without us feeling uncomfortable; personal distance generally takes in good friends and family; social distance is the distance we adopt with people whom we know only fairly well; public distance is the space of, say, a teacher and a class of students. With dating, it's usually good to begin at a personal distance and move closer when you're ready.

HOW MUCH SPACE?
People's exact preferences can vary from culture to culture and individual to individual, but these are some good yardsticks to follow.

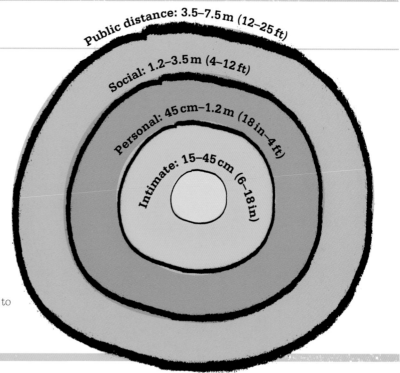

Public distance: 3.5–7.5 m (12–25 ft)

Social: 1.2–3.5 m (4–12 ft)

Personal: 45 cm–1.2 m (18 in–4 ft)

Intimate: 15–45 cm (6–18 in)

I'M SO EMBARRASSED!
HOW TO KEEP YOUR COOL

Your date is attractive, the evening is going well … but you've just made a duff joke or noticed that your skirt is tucked into your underpants. How do you stop a faux pas from ruining the rendezvous?

Let's face it: no one gets through life without sometimes making a fool of him- or herself. If we have reasonable levels of self-esteem, we can usually get over it – but what happens if we trip up in the middle of a date with someone we really want to impress?

Do I look all that ridiculous?
In reality, how much do other people judge us when we do something embarrassing? It depends on the observer, of course, and on just how big an idiot we've made of ourselves, but it also depends on the similarities between audience and idiot. A study in the *European Journal of Social Psychology* found that people were more likely to spot embarrassment in people of similar nationality and status to themselves; it appears that when we see someone as beneath us, we assume they feel less stupid if they do something foolish, perhaps

🔍 WHAT IS EMBARRASSMENT?

Feeling embarrassed is an automatic response to revealing an apparent flaw in the presence of others. The emotion is registered in a part of the brain called the "pregenual anterior cingulate cortex" (PACC). In tests at Berkeley, California, volunteers watched videos of themselves singing "My Girl" *a capella*, and showed increased activity in their PACC region, combined with an elevated heart rate, sweaty palms, and unhappy remarks about how bad they looked. There's little we can do to avoid feeling embarrassed: it happens without our willing it and is a physical as well as an emotional response to stress.

because we think they have less far to fall. In a sense, there's some good news here: feeling embarrassed can be a way to test your date's opinion of you. If they notice that you're feeling silly, it's a sign that they see you as their equal: even if they do think you've done something a bit dumb, they also see you as "one of us". If, however, they don't notice you're embarrassed, this may be a sign you should be on the alert: are they treating you like an equal? Everyone does embarrassing things sometimes; you want to date someone who has empathy for that.

Embarrassment versus shame
The key to managing an awkward moment is to draw a distinction between embarrassment – the instantaneous reaction that makes you blush or cringe when you think others see a flaw in you – and shame, the negative assessment you have of

yourself that can be hard to shake off. When you feel embarrassed, you can balance the "flaw" by reminding yourself of a broader, more positive image of yourself. That way, the "flaw" becomes just a minor setback and an indication that you're only human. If you tend to struggle with feelings of shame, then it is important to work on self-acceptance and self-compassion (see pages 54–57).

We'll never be embarrassment-proof, but if our self-image doesn't depend on denying our capacity to be sometimes clumsy or unwise, a fleeting faux pas needn't ruin a date: when it doesn't contradict how we already see ourselves, it may feel silly but it doesn't call our identity into question. With self-acceptance and self-compassion, we can see ourselves as valuable people who make the odd mistake – and in accepting that, we get better at surviving the odd goof.

 ## HOW TO KEEP CALM AND CARRY ON

✔ **Is blushing bad?** Not at all. "Blushes are very useful for conveying apologies," says UK psychologist Ray Crozier. If your face is burning, try not to worry: it may actually defuse the situation by showing you didn't mean any harm.

✔ **Laugh it off.** Did you really put your foot in it? Make a joke. Many of us will laugh at the discomfiture of others, but if you can laugh at your own, you are effectively putting yourself in the audience rather than in the spotlight: you and your date can laugh together at your slip-up, which means that you're allied against the embarrassment rather than separated by it. A sense of humour is always attractive (see pages 50–51), so take the opportunity to share a laugh.

✔ **'Fess up.** Okay, so you spilled coffee all over your lap. Since you can't hide it, just say straight out, "Oh, I'm so embarrassed!" But here's the key: only say it once. We tend to take people on their own estimation, so the more you act like there's something wrong, the more your date will feel there is. Admitting to being embarrassed shows that you're candid; moving on from your embarrassment shows that you can handle little setbacks … and who wouldn't want to date an honest, well-adjusted person?

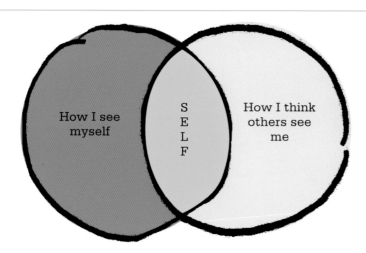

How I see myself

S E L F

How I think others see me

IN THE SPOTLIGHT
Is your goof really that obvious? Very possibly not. We are prone to what psychology professor Thomas Gilovich calls "the spotlight effect". In studies at Cornell University in 2000, his research volunteers greatly overestimated how many fellow students noticed the "embarrassing" design on their T-shirts. Our flaws, in other words, glare far brighter in our self-image, and in how we think others see us, than they do in the image others really see.

FIVE ACID TESTS

HOW TO ASSESS YOUR NEW DATE

Sometimes little things can tell us a lot. Here are a few situations to consider as good indicators of a date's attitudes towards love and commitment: watch for their reactions and see what you learn.

✓ DO THEY CALL WHEN THEY SAY THEY WILL?

If someone promises they'll call you tonight but waits a week, look to their attachment style (see pages 16–19). A couple of late calls may not mean much – anyone can get shy or busy – but if they make a habit of it, you could be dealing with either an avoidant person who is creating pre-emptive distance, or an anxious person who is afraid of annoying you by being "needy".

If you point out they keep calling late and they get nervous and apologetic, you're probably looking at an anxious person: they may turn into a loving and loyal partner if you're comfortable giving regular reassurance, but they may continue to need that. Or if their response is to shrug it off and get defensive or self-righteous if you push, you're probably looking at an avoidant person: they may be fun, but they may not be looking for intimacy. Each can be fine, but these are long-term patterns – and whatever the reason for their behaviour, keep in mind that it is not acceptable if it upsets or bothers you.

If, on the other hand, your new prospect tends to do what they said they'd do, there's a good chance you're looking at a secure person who values connection. A person who keeps small promises early on is more likely to keep big promises later.

THE FIVE-STEP TEST

Out walking with your date on a busy street, fall about five paces behind them. Then wait and see how long it takes them to notice and turn around to look for you.

If they don't turn fairly soon, then you're probably staring at the back of a person who is using a "deactivating strategy" – detaching themselves from feelings of closeness so they don't get too emotionally involved with you. Of course, everyone gets distracted sometimes, but if they do it a lot, walking may not be the only time they "need their space".

If, on the other hand, your date notices you aren't there and glances back to check, how do they react? Are they annoyed you couldn't keep up? Bothered they've lost their audience? Worried you're shunning them? Or subtly inviting you to join them? Keep your eyes open for the date who welcomes you into their space as a valued companion.

 TELL THEM YOU DON'T LIKE…

… their favourite book, movie, sport, or hobby – not if you actually do, of course, and not in a rude way. But if your date is into something that doesn't appeal to you, try telling them in a friendly way that it's really not your thing.

This could save you a lifetime of tedium sitting through sports or films you hate, but the real reason is to see how your date reacts. If they consider ball games or romcoms a dealbreaker, it's best to know now. More importantly, the best partner is one who doesn't take differences personally.

Look for someone who thinks, "Hey, let's compare notes on this – it's a chance to learn more about this interesting person." Even if they don't convert you to the joys of beekeeping or linedancing, you may come to enjoy their enthusiasm and feel happy in your mutual acceptance of each other's quirky tastes and interests.

 MAKE A PERSONAL COMMENT

Nothing too touchy – "You know, your nose is huge" is never a good line – but if they always order the spiciest item on the menu or their clothes have a bohemian flair, then try a neutral question or remark about that, and listen to their reaction. Are they a bit full of themselves and apt to pontificate on how all their choices are the best choices? Are they insecure and assume they're being criticized? Or are they confident in themselves and happy to own their preferences?

However, be aware that if you keep offending dates with your comments, the problem might be your presentation, not their attitude!

 OWN UP TO YOUR WORRIES

Have they said something that hurt your feelings or done something that made you feel insecure? Do you want to invite them home, but your place is an embarrassing mess today? Say so.

If you're going to be in a relationship with this person, they'll have to learn you're not perfect. How they handle your wounded feelings or embarrassment will tell you a lot about what sort of partner they'd make: a kind and understanding person is kind and understanding from the start, and your admitting those flaws is a chance for your date to show how nice they can be.

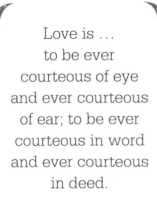

Love is … to be ever courteous of eye and ever courteous of ear; to be ever courteous in word and ever courteous in deed.

Confucius
Ancient Chinese philosopher

THE EMOTIONS DO NOT DESERVE BEING PUT INTO OPPOSITION WITH "INTELLIGENCE". THE EMOTIONS ARE THEMSELVES A HIGHER ORDER OF INTELLIGENCE

ORVAL HOBART MOWRER (1907–1982), PSYCHOLOGIST, PROFESSOR, AND PRESIDENT OF THE AMERICAN PSYCHOLOGICAL ASSOCIATION

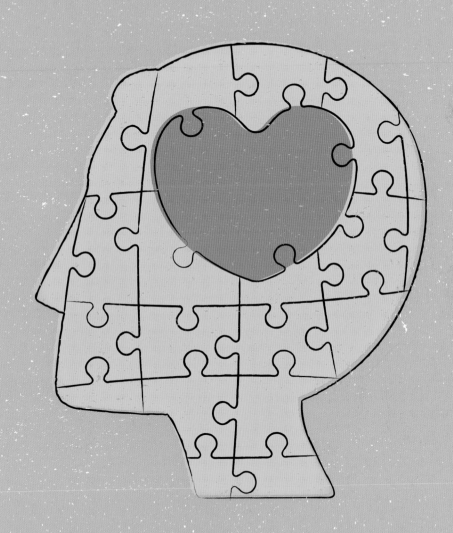

EMOTIONAL INTELLIGENCE
WHAT IT IS AND WHY IT MATTERS

No one wants an insensitive partner, so emotional intelligence is a much-prized asset in the quest to find and keep a good relationship. What can we do to hone our skills and improve our chances?

Intelligence is not a single quality of mind, but instead a series of multiple abilities overlapping in greater or lesser degrees. While researchers may draw the boundaries in slightly different places (see the chart opposite), the basic premise is consistent: understanding and coping with emotion are a form of intelligence in their own right. In effect, an "intelligent" person has a brain that can recognize and manage information particularly well, while an "emotionally intelligent" person has an advanced facility for recognizing and managing feelings, both their own and other people's.

Emotionally intelligent dating

We'd all rather date someone who is emotionally intelligent than someone who is emotionally stupid, but how big a factor is it in romantic happiness?

Research published in the *American Journal of Family Therapy* in 2014 found that emotionally intelligent people were more likely to report happiness in their romantic relationships and to have satisfied partners. Finding an emotionally intelligent person isn't a cure-all: a study in the *European Journal of Personality* in 2011 found that the happiest relationships involved both partners having emotional intelligence. If you suspect your own emotional intelligence isn't the best, is there anything you can do about it?

Getting emotionally smarter

Age does, apparently, bring wisdom: a study by Six Seconds, a global EQ network, found that people do grow in emotional intelligence as the years go by. Rather than wait for that to happen, though, what next?

Different aspects of emotional intelligence can be easier or harder to learn. A 2003 study in Texas found that training programmes could help workers raise their interpersonal skills – negotiation and etiquette – by around 50 per cent. That compares to a rise of around 35 per cent reported by occupational stress management programmes, while a study in 2008 found that cognitive behavioural programmes appeared to have the best results. These were all studies of workplace rather than romantic programmes, but the data supports the idea that practice combined with honest feedback does reap rewards.

Your best bet, psychology suggests, is twofold: practise your own emotional intelligence, and favour suitors who seem emotionally smart. If you can keep in mind the qualities you need when meeting new people (see opposite for examples), you may be better equipped to spot the good prospects on shorter acquaintance.

50%

Training programmes can help workers **raise interpersonal skills** by as much as **half**.

MULTIPLE THEORIES

Theories of different kinds of intelligence are constantly being adapted by different psychologists and writers. Here are three of the best known:

Howard Gardner	Multiple intelligences	Skills
Harvard psychologist Howard Gardner's original list in 1983 proposed seven types of intelligence. In terms of romance, the last two are probably the most important – though bodily-kinaesthetic can help when it comes to sexual chemistry.	Linguistic	Sensitivity to language, and ability to learn and use it.
	Logical-mathematical	Scientific and numerical analysis.
	Musical	Recognizing, appreciating, and creating musical patterns.
	Bodily-kinaesthetic	Judging position and distance.
	Visual-spatial	"Hands-on" intelligence, as with an artist or athlete.
	Interpersonal	Social skills and the ability to relate to others.
	Intrapersonal	Self-awareness; insight into your feelings and motives.

Mayer and Salovey	Four branches	Skills
American psychologists John Mayer and Peter Salovey elaborated on Gardner's theories to list four basic "branches" or abilities that create emotional intelligence – all of which can help in romantic relationships.	Perceiving emotions	Identifying emotion, in yourself, others, and the arts.
	Facilitating thought	Using emotion to help you think and communicate.
	Understanding emotions	Grasping how emotions combine and change, and what that means in human relationships.
	Managing emotions	Using and moderating feelings to promote understanding and growth.

Daniel Goleman	Top five	Skills
Daniel Goleman's bestselling book *Emotional Intelligence* identifies five categories, all applicable to romance.	Self-awareness	Understanding your own feelings.
	Self-regulation	Managing your emotions effectively.
	Self-motivation	Directing your emotions to productive ends.
	Empathy	Appreciating and sharing the feelings of others.
	Social skills	Communicating and dealing with other people.

SPOTTING A SERIAL DATER

WHO THEY ARE AND WHY THEY DO IT

If you're looking for a committed relationship, there's a certain kind of person you probably know from painful experience: the hot-and-cold, not-ready-to-be-tied-down partner who keeps you on the back foot. This is the avoidant attachment style described on pages 16–21. Avoidant types may need love but they fear abandonment, and try to shut down their emotions before they get hurt.

As the US population percentages show below, most people are secure, but about one in four are avoidants, who go through a lot of relationships. If you're a secure type and you find the fun of being with someone outweighs their need for emotional distance, you may have a perfectly successful relationship – but if you want more and you meet an avoidant person in their gadding about phase, you stand a good chance of getting hurt. How do you recognize an avoidant person before you get too interested?

They're charming, they're good-looking, they're a lot of fun, they really seem to like you … and the next thing you know they've dropped out of touch and moved on. What's going on?

SPOTTING THE SIGNS

While an avoidant attachment style can be anything from a freewheeling party animal to a tight-wound hermit, there are certain traits in common:

- **They disparage intimacy.** You want to spend time together and they tell you not to be "needy". Or your best friend is engaged and they make cracks about "shackles". Avoidants warn you not to expect closeness, but often in subtle ways to avoid you "making a scene".

- **They treat making contact as a power play.** "When can I call?" is something everyone wonders about, but avoidants may feel you're needy and that showing any interest makes them weak.

- **They dance around closeness.** There are moments when it feels you're connecting, but somehow these never turn into a deeper bond. Avoidants need connection but it makes them nervous; small doses are all they can handle.

- **They start to open up a bit, then quickly close down again.** For a secure or anxious person, it's natural to know about a partner's feelings and past, but avoidants don't like to reveal too much.

- **They don't seem upset when talking about an upsetting past.** Not all avoidants had bad parents, but avoidant attachment comes from the expectation of your needs not being met. Of course many people get over bad experiences, but non-avoidants acknowledge they were bad. If someone doesn't seem to feel the emotions you'd expect when telling an emotional story, they may not want to feel much for you either.

- **They don't treat you better once you're together.** They may even start treating you worse. When avoidants fall in love, the "pursuit" stage is fine so long as the intimacy isn't there yet. Once it looks likely, you're no longer a goal to them, you're a threat.

- **They give you warnings you don't deserve.** A partner who says they need their "freedom" or "space" when you never encroach on either is trying to stop you getting close. If they say this early on, they're already thinking you'll take it away.

- **They act superior in a conflict.** Watch out for the person who acts above you because you're "getting all emotional" and they aren't. Not agreeing with you is one thing; looking down on emotion is another.

- **You feel like you're in a contest, with their affection as the prize.** And you don't know the rules, or they keep changing. An avoidant can be "my way or the highway" when it comes to love: if things get too much, they'd rather leave, physically or emotionally. That makes them able to drive a hard bargain – which may not be how you want to approach a relationship.

- **They have a romantic ideal you can't live up to.** They "never got over" their ex, or dream of the "perfect" love (which you can't fulfil). Insisting on the impossible is a reliable way to shut down their feelings for someone real.

What if you are both avoidant?

Avoidant people aren't monsters: they're just people who need love, are worried about getting hurt, and feel safer depending on themselves. Often avoidant people don't mean to cause pain, but their inner conflict can leave a partner confused. If you are avoidant, make it a goal to find someone you can trust, and then try opening up: once you've taken the chance, it can turn out for the best. Watch out, though for dates who show signs of an anxious attachment style: anxious-avoidant couples can be a terrible combination, so see pages 148–149 for what to expect.

It wouldn't be like this if...

One common avoidant method for keeping things low-key is fixing on a "romantic ideal" (see below left). If you're dating someone who acts this way and hints that things would be different if only you were better, don't take it personally: they're trying to manage their own feelings, and it's not really about you.

If you're the avoidant one, though, and you know you act this way but you tell yourself that with the right person you wouldn't have to – don't listen to those thoughts. There's no such thing as a perfect person, and any partner's flaws and needs will start to trouble you eventually. The thing to do at that stage is remind yourself you're feeling anxiety and focus on communication and self-calming: the problem may not be that you're with the wrong person, and you can fix it without ending the relationship if you try.

SOMEONE LIKE YOU?

WHEN QUALITIES IN COMMON HELP, AND WHEN THEY DON'T

Birds of a feather flock together, or opposites attract? When it comes to picking a partner, which of the two old sayings is closer to the truth? Does variety add to the spice of life, or is compatibility the key?

THE BIG FIVE

Studies have identified five dimensions that form the building blocks of personality, each representing a broad spectrum of traits. Your personality is a unique blend from across the Big Five.

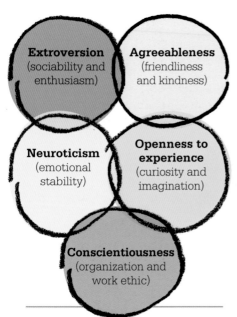

Extroversion (sociability and enthusiasm)

Agreeableness (friendliness and kindness)

Neuroticism (emotional stability)

Openness to experience (curiosity and imagination)

Conscientiousness (organization and work ethic)

Shared interests and tastes can help, of course, while a new partner may bring new interests and tastes into our life, but when it comes to relationship happiness, our basic attitudes are what really count.

Complex minds?

Are you a complicated thinker, or do you like things more clear-cut? Would you call yourself an intellectual, or do you prefer things down-to-earth and basic? The odds are that whatever you answer, your best romantic bet is someone similar to you. A 1997 study in the *Journal of Constructivist Psychology* compared people's "cognitive complexity" in three areas: social, task-oriented, and intellectual. The results? People tended to go for people like themselves: "HC" (high complexity) subjects were more attracted to HC people than "LC" (low complexity), while LC subjects rated LC people higher than the HC people

did. Birds of a feather, it would seem, though there was a variation: LC people showed an unexpected (and somewhat unrequited) attraction to complex people.

The conclusion seems to be that when picking partners, we want someone at least as complex as ourselves, if not more so. It may also be a hint that if you're considering casting your eye over someone much more complex than you, you might do better to give them a miss and look for someone more straightforward like you.

Matching temperaments?

Do you want someone whose disposition is like yours, or someone different? It may sound vain to say you want someone similar, but if you do, you're in the majority: a 2014 study from the *Journal of Research in Personality* found that a major predictor of romantic satisfaction was perceiving your partner as like yourself. The personality qualities tested in this case were psychology's remarkably universal "Big Five": extroversion, agreeableness, conscientiousness, neuroticism, and openness to experience (see left).

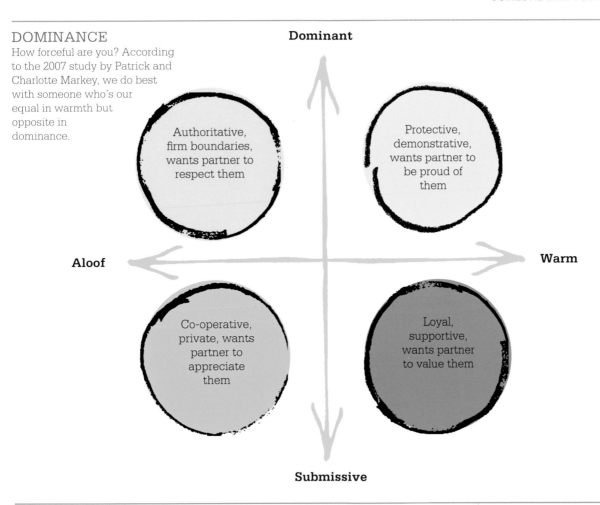

DOMINANCE

How forceful are you? According to the 2007 study by Patrick and Charlotte Markey, we do best with someone who's our equal in warmth but opposite in dominance.

Dominant

Authoritative, firm boundaries, wants partner to respect them

Protective, demonstrative, wants partner to be proud of them

Aloof

Warm

Co-operative, private, wants partner to appreciate them

Loyal, supportive, wants partner to value them

Submissive

When it comes to the fundamentals, it seems we mostly want harmony.

There is a quality this study didn't test, though, which psychologists call "dominance": how forceful a personality you have, and how aggressive you are in going after what you want. A study in 2007 by psychologists Patrick and Charlotte Markey tested couples for dominance and also for warmth: some people like lots of affection and some prefer a little dignified distance. The results in this case suggested that difference can sometimes help: the happiest couples had a similar level of warmth, but a dissimilar level of dominance –

perhaps because one accommodating partner saves on needless conflict.

Want to agree?

When it comes to harmony, the key may be this: we may or may not want someone exactly like ourselves, but we do want someone who cares what we think. In 2013, *the Journal of Social Psychology* described an experiment in which people met a stranger, discussed social issues about which they disagreed, and then rated their attractiveness after receiving the psychologists' feedback on whether the stranger's attitudes had shifted closer to theirs. In fact the

feedback was false – the researchers made it up to reflect different degrees of attitude adjustment. Result: the more someone appeared to change their mind after a disagreement, the more attractive they were rated.

In the search for love, it seems that compatible personalities are a great starting point – though compatible doesn't always mean identical – but that everybody likes a partner who takes their opinions seriously.

If you can find a person who suits your disposition and then show them your great listening skills (see pages 106–107), you could be on the road to happiness.

COUNTING THE YEARS

DO AGE GAPS REALLY MATTER?

When it comes to dating a much older or younger partner, there's no getting around it: people are going to comment. Even open-minded people will probably sound a note of caution. Do they have a point?

Toy boy, arm candy, cradle snatcher: there are a lot of nasty names for people who date someone years older or younger. With such a background of social disapproval, you may find yourself hesitating to date someone out of your own generation, even if the two of you hit it off: do you have enough in common, are you sure they're not just taking advantage, and is this really healthy?

Sounding the warnings

Why do intergenerational romances have such a bad reputation? Part of it may simply be the atavistic part of our brains telling us that relationships are for producing children. A so-called "May-December" couple's reproductive peaks don't align, so bystanders may instinctively feel they shouldn't be together.

This isn't very logical, of course: both men and women can have children later in life, and even if they don't, there are more reasons to be together and more ways to be a family than traditional childbearing.

½ + 7?

A proverbial piece of advice – often attributed to **French entertainer Maurice Chevalier** – is that you shouldn't date anyone younger than **half your age plus seven.** He didn't always take his own advice, though: he is said to have dated a woman of 36 when he was 23 and a woman of 32 when he was 64.

There's also a less primitive concern: different generations are not balanced in what they bring to the relationship. The younger partner brings youth, a valuable sexual asset, while the older partner brings greater experience and maturity, and often more money and status as well. The fear that one is exploiting another – that the nubile body or larger bank balance is the only thing your partner sees in you – will loom large in some minds.

Getting it right

If you look at the statistics of age-gap relationships, the outlook isn't nearly so dire. In 2008, an American study of heterosexual couples found that the happiest relationships of all were "women-older" ones, whereas a study of Canadian divorce rates in 1990–91 found that the couples least likely to divorce were those with a much older husband! Either way, couples who commit despite an age gap may turn out to be very stable and contented.

Is there a key to success? Probably the best answer is to be aware of your differences as something to balance rather than exploit. Sex columnist Dan Savage formulated the famous "campsite rule" for dating younger partners: as with visiting a campsite, you should leave your partner "better off than you found them", with "no STIs, no fertilized eggs, no restraining orders, no emotional trauma, and with improved sexual skills". Of course, this is a pretty good rule for any relationship (unless "fertilized eggs" are something you want), but as long as you're sure your partner likes you for yourself and not for your age, there's no reason not to give the relationship a try. Statistics suggest that if you can make it work, it could work very well indeed.

> { ... this maiden, who was called May ... shall be married to this January }
>
> **Geoffrey Chaucer**
> in *The Canterbury Tales – The Merchant's Prologue*

 BRIDGING THE GAP

If you think you've met the right person, whether older or younger, a few tips to help keep the relationship happy:

1 **Know what appeals.** If they were your age, would you still love them?

2 **Accept the cultural differences.** Dating across generations can be like dating across nationalities or cultures. Don't be threatened by that; it's part of who you both are.

3 **Be each other's rock.** Unless you're very lucky, friends and family will comment. If the relationship lasts and clearly makes you both happy, they'll probably stop – but be sure you can support each other in the meantime.

4 **Don't obsess about it.** You're both likely to get self-conscious if you dwell on the age gap too much. Be together and focus on other things.

WHAT THE STATISTICS SAY

Most people marry someone close to their own age – one third marry someone up to a year older or younger, according to US population data for 2013. See below for the many statistical outliers: there's no reason your relationship couldn't be among them.

Age Gap	Husbands	Wives
2–3 years older	20.4% of husbands are 2–3 years older than their wives.	6.5% of wives are 2–3 years older than their husbands.
4–9 years older	24.9%	6%
10–19 years older	6.4%	1.3%
20+ years older	1%	0.3%

WORTH A SECOND DATE?
WHO SHOULD YOU SEE AGAIN?

We often feel that if attraction or connection don't happen at once, they aren't going to happen. If we stick to that in our dating, and expect to find love at first sight (or on a first date), could we be missing out?

Everyone has their own idea of Mr or Ms Right, and how detailed that picture is varies from person to person. Most of us know that no real individual is going to match our mental image precisely: instead, we tend to take an interest in people based on whether or not it "feels right". How far do we trust our feelings as a guide?

If someone turns out to be a real boor on your first date, there's no need to give them a second chance. Have you ever dated someone, though, who seemed perfectly okay – attractive, nice, interesting – but somehow you just couldn't feel a spark? If so, did you decide it wasn't worth trying again with a second date? The trouble is, what we tend to associate with the "spark" and what will actually make us happy in a relationship may not be the same thing.

Promising, or just familiar?
Suppose you want a deep connection, but have a history of dating people who are emotionally unavailable – or you love your work and friends, but always seem to get partners who want your undivided attention 24/7. You don't want these kinds of relationship, but they seem to keep happening. Maybe you've got some unresolved issues that steer you in the wrong direction (see pages 28–29), or maybe you've just had bad luck: either way, your love life keeps running into the same problems. If you've met someone new, your dearest hope is that this time it will be different.

Here's the twist: if it's different, it will feel different – and because it doesn't feel like the last few times you got interested in someone, you might assume you aren't interested this time.

Exciting or scary?
Falling for someone who isn't a safe haven for us (see pages 16–19) can be unnerving. The rush of feeling is hard to sort out: we feel thrilled, hopeful, scared, and unhappy all at the same time – sometimes so intensely that we can barely think straight. If you have a somewhat anxious attachment style, you're particularly prone to this (see pages 148–149), but even if you don't, the uncertainty carries a major adrenalin rush.

If you're used to the adrenalin, meeting someone predictable can feel a bit dull. They're interesting to talk to, but they don't keep you guessing – and if you're not guessing, you assume you're not intrigued. But if you want a long-term relationship,

---

🔍 FAKE IT TILL YOU MAKE IT?

Psychology professor John Wiseman asked some Edinburgh speed daters to "fake" attraction. About 20 per cent of the control group (who hadn't faked anything) said they'd like to meet their speed dates again – as did 45 per cent of the fakers. It seems faking it can more than double your chances!

LEARNING FROM EXPERIENCE

1 **If our expectations of love** are based on people who aren't very good for us – say we've had bad luck with partners or we grew up in an environment full of tension – we may not know how to deal with feeling calm:

2 **If you're puzzled by the lack of a spark** on a first date, try going through this sequence instead, to see whether your new date is worth a second chance:

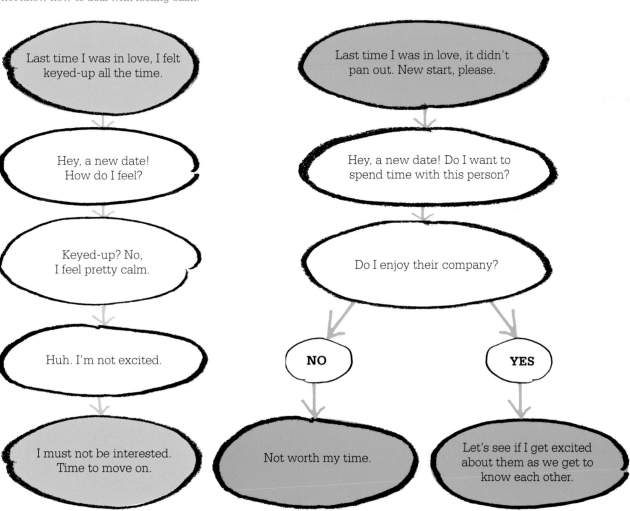

Last time I was in love, I felt keyed-up all the time.

↓

Hey, a new date! How do I feel?

↓

Keyed-up? No, I feel pretty calm.

↓

Huh. I'm not excited.

↓

I must not be interested. Time to move on.

Last time I was in love, it didn't pan out. New start, please.

↓

Hey, a new date! Do I want to spend time with this person?

↓

Do I enjoy their company?

↙ ↘

NO   **YES**

↓   ↓

Not worth my time.   Let's see if I get excited about them as we get to know each other.

---

bear in mind that a baseline of predictability is a good thing: you should be able to predict reliably that someone will treat you well. None of us really wants someone who may disappear for weeks or lose their temper without warning – we want someone we can trust.

Think twice

If your first date goes okay but doesn't seem very exciting, it's probably worth going to a second. That's not a major commitment, and sometimes people grow more fascinating over time. The key is to distinguish between someone who

doesn't excite you because they're a dull person and someone who doesn't excite you because they don't drag you through the familiar sleepless nights and heartache. The first type doesn't merit a third date – but the second could turn out to be the most romantic thing ever to happen to you.

JUGGLING PROSPECTS

WHEN THERE'S MORE THAN ONE PERSON ON THE HORIZON

Sometimes, more than one attractive person comes along at once – especially if you're Internet dating. Can you try seeing them all, or should you make a choice up front? Is there an ethical way to multiple date?

If you meet more than one attractive prospect, you may find yourself caught between making the wrong choice and losing them all through delay. Can you try a period of multiple dating? That depends on two things: culture and context.

Any cultural assumptions?
How acceptable it is to date multiple people depends a great deal on your culture: your nationality and religion, but also the subcultures you move in. In some circles, a date clearly marks the start of an exclusive relationship. In others, early dating is an audition process and no exclusivity should be assumed until you agree otherwise. So ask yourself: what are the default assumptions of your own culture? And what are the assumptions of the person or people you'd like to date?

How did you meet?
The context in which you met is also important. If you know a person through mutual friends and you find you're growing closer, the implied commitment is greater than when you like someone's dating site profile and exchange a few chatty e-mails. If you are keen on one or more colleagues, be *extremely* careful: office romances are touchy at the best of times (see pages 70–71), and the issues multiply with more than one romance in view.

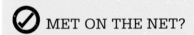

⊘ MET ON THE NET?

How can you know whether someone is serious about you or still auditioning other candidates? Log onto the dating site and check their profile status: only assume it's exclusive once you've both taken your profiles offline.

RULE NUMBER ONE

Be honest. You don't have to disclose your whole social schedule on a first date, but you do need to be fair once things start to progress. Here are some useful phrases:

- **I'd like us to get to know each other** before we commit to making it exclusive. Are you okay with that?

- **How would you feel about dating non-exclusively** for a while? That way we can both be sure we're picking the right person.

- **I feel more comfortable dating non-exclusively** and taking things slowly until we're both sure. What would work for you?

The key is to make it clear that their feelings matter too. Start as you mean to go on, and communicate openly.

BOUNDARIES, PEOPLE

If you are seeing several people, keep some space between your dates, and remember these key points:

1 **Don't go to the same places** with different people. You don't want the waiters, bartenders, or regulars making comments.

2 **Schedule your dates on separate days.** Rushing from one person to another means that any time with one cuts into time with another, which isn't fair on them. Give enough time to each date so they get your full attention.

3 **When booking dates** with them, don't say, "Not Friday, I've got another date then." It's one thing to know your date may be seeing other people; it's another if they rub it in your face. Just say, "I can't do Friday" and suggest another time.

4 **Keep friends and family out of it.** You'll spare yourself interference, and avoid implying you're more committed than you are. Meeting friends and family is bringing someone into your life: wait until you're sure you want to do that.

BREAKING THE NEWS

One of your suitors is the cream of the crop and you're ready to commit? Time to tell the others – top tips include:

- **Tell them face to face;** it's more respectful and shows you're prepared to make the effort.

- **Be affirming:** "I've decided to get serious with someone else, but I've had a wonderful time with you and I really hope all goes well for you." They've done nothing wrong, so be nice.

- **Respect their right to be upset.** They may take it casually, but they may feel like it's a break-up. Their disappointment is a compliment. Let them feel whatever they feel.

- **If you'd like to stay friends,** don't make the offer without talking to your newly committed partner first. If your soon-to-be-ex-date doesn't want to be friends that's their decision, so don't push.

- **Get it over with.** It's only fair to everyone concerned, and signals your sincerity to your new partner.

Looking to change?

If you have a history of getting into "wrong" relationships and want to change, a period of multiple dating can be helpful. Sometimes love takes a while to get going; if you're dating around, there'll be less temptation to panic and throw over the nice ones before you've really given them the chance to win your heart.

As a general rule of thumb, the more opportunities you have to get to know someone *non*-romantically, the more commitment will be implied by

a date. If you have to go on a date to get to know someone, multiple dates may be reasonable. If you can get to know them by going to the same parties or chatting over the water cooler, a date implies some kind of transition. Multiple dating can be complicated, and some of us may be better suited to it than others. But if you can handle it without exhausting yourself or misleading your partners, it can be a good way to build up your confidence and be sure that whoever you finally pick is the best choice.

3:14

Some research suggests that on average, **men** know they're **falling in love** after **three dates;** for **women**, it takes **14.**

SAYING IT WITH FLOWERS

GIFT-GIVING AND WHAT IT MEANS

We all love a little treat, and when it comes from someone we care about, it means all the more. Sometimes, though, it puts us under pressure. What's the best way to handle gifts in a relationship?

On the surface, a bunch of flowers or a box of chocolates seem such simple things. When it comes to gifts, though, there's actually a complicated social dance going on: how we give and receive can have a tremendous significance in our relationships.

Exchange rates

When someone gives you a gift, how do you feel? Delighted, hopefully, if the gift is a nice one – but there's also a slight niggle at the back of your mind: now you probably have to give them something at some point. We tend to feel that a one-sided gift creates an imbalance in the relationship that we need to correct – not necessarily with the same kind of gift, but with something of roughly equal value, either in cost or in effort.

If that all sounds a bit mercenary, think again – it's actually a core component of non-mercenary relationships. Anthropologist Laura Bohannan described a good example: arriving to stay at a Tiv community in Nigeria, she found that the local women gave her various small gifts, such as a chicken or a few tomatoes. She was unsure how to respond until two new friends explained: she should, at a discreet interval, give gifts in return. But her gifts couldn't be exactly equivalent in value. They

> The manner of giving is worth more than the gift.
>
> **Pierre Corneille**
> French playwright,
> in *The Liar*, 1644

$18.6 billion

According to the National Retail Federation, in 2013 Americans spent **$18.6 billion** on **Valentine's Day gifts**, averaging $131 per person (topped by $169 on Mother's Day).

51%

After cards, the most popular gift on Valentine's Day is **confectionary** (51 per cent), followed by **flowers** and **dining** (each 36 per cent), and **jewellery** (19 per cent).

233 million roses

… were grown for US valentines in 2013. Some **73 per cent** of all valentine bouquets are **bought by men**, while 14 per cent of women **buy themselves** flowers.

---

had to be worth either slightly more or slightly less. That way, the "debt" would remain slightly uneven no matter who was giving what, and the amicable exchange would have to continue indefinitely. Giving an exactly equivalent gift was a sign you no longer wanted to be friends.

Nor is that unique to Nigeria's Tiv community. In every culture, psychologists observe a difference between what they call "social norms" and "market norms" – gift-exchange relationships in which the reward is a sense of connection – and closed financial interactions such as a purchase in a shop. In fact, evidence suggests we may do more for a social connection than for a financial reward. In research by James Heyman and Dan Ariely, published in 2004 in *Psychological Science*, volunteers gave up on an impossible task more quickly when they were being paid than when they were doing it for free: the ones whose reward was to feel they were helping out put in the most effort. We are evolved to want to feel connected, and a sense of favour-doing is one of the most powerful connectors.

Love is…

What does this have to do with romance? The key point is this: unless you're looking for an unequal relationship, the presents you give each other are best seen as an equal exchange. When you're trying to balance the relationship, gifts can become a subtle language to communicate your sense of each other's value, not a bidding war.

It's for this reason that you're advised to be careful of a suitor who presses huge favours or expensive gifts on you without your consent: fundamentally, they may be trying to create a sense of indebtedness, which could signal abusive motives (see pages 156–157).

What you want is a relationship where each of you is sensitive to your partner's tastes – a thoughtful present can say a lot about how closely you observe and dearly value someone – and the mutual exchange becomes a dance of subtle, attentive reciprocity. That's how you know that respect and appreciation are alive and well in your romance.

WHAT DO YOU TAKE ME FOR?

We may do more for a "social norm" than a "market one" (see left), but be careful: if a social norm is treated like a market one (dinner, say, in return for sex), it becomes a market exchange, and probably you aren't paying enough. If you assume buying dinner means anything more, you've treated the social norm like a market one – as a payment, not a kindness bestowed to further a social relationship – and your date will not forgive you. If you go further and tell them what the dinner cost, it's a good way to get slapped in the face for implying someone's favours can be "bought".

CHAPTER 4

ESTABLISHING THE RELATIONSHIP

FROM ATTRACTION TO COMMITMENT

FAST TRACK, SLOW TRACK
GETTING THE PACE RIGHT FOR YOU

Sometimes a date just feels right, but sometimes you need a little time to make up your mind. Does slow and steady win the race for you, or do you see no reason to delay a good thing?

Sometimes you're totally in love and ready to move forward right away. Sometimes, though, you need a little time to be sure. If your partner feels the same way, then all is well – but how do you make sure the pace is right for both of you?

Getting attached
Our pace of commitment is guided to some extent by our attachment style (see pages 16–19). People with an anxious attachment style are hyper-aware of any hint of rejection and feel most comfortable with regular reassurance. The early stages of a relationship, when rejection is still a distinct possibility, can be a difficult time for them – thrilling, but stressful.

Reassurance can be as simple as "I've been looking forward to this evening". If you are anxious, be upfront and ask for such assurances: the right person for you is someone who appreciates the directness. If you're dating someone anxious, remember they can sometimes panic and be demanding: telling them to back off will probably only agitate them further. If you really do like them, tell them; it will make everything else easier.

On the other hand, if you're more of an anxious person who is trying to break old habits after a string of madly exciting but ultimately unhappy relationships (see pages 28–29), you may be deliberately choosing a slower pace. If so, congratulations – and remember not to transform your fear of rejection for being too "needy" into fear of rejection for being too distant. A person who likes you won't vanish just because you slow things down a little.

How slow is too slow?
People towards the avoidant end of the attachment spectrum are the commitment phobes of the dating world: a slow path to intimacy – or

even a slow path to not-too-much-intimacy – is their comfort zone. If you're dating an avoidant person, remember that hesitating to get close isn't necessarily hesitating about you: they have their limits, and it will take a lot to change them.

If you are the avoidant one, be as fair as possible. You have the right to your space, but if you need to ask for it, make it clear that this is your issue, not your partner's fault. Pulling away can worry even secure people, so if you really do like this person, give what reassurance you can. It will probably gain you more space in the end: a worried partner makes more demands than a calm one!

Opening up

The pacesetters of a relationship aren't all obvious. A commitment is usually clear, but sharing a painful secret, for example, is also a key marker of growing intimacy. If you're anxious, you may rush to confide everything at once, which can make your partner feel more like a therapist than an equal. In the early stages, don't forget that friends, too, can help calm an agitated attachment system (see pages 38–39).

On the other hand, how a partner reacts to important disclosures is absolutely vital in establishing intimacy: responding with empathy and interest can do more to keep the relationship moving forward than any amount of mini-breaks and bouquets.

A comfortable pace is based on mutual respect for each other's needs. Open communication of those needs is vital: if you can understand and accept each other in the early stages, you're laying an excellent foundation for the future.

✏️ YES, THIS IS A BIG DEAL!

What counts as a major sign of commitment? A survey of a thousand heterosexual women in the UK found that some of the top ten "not in the first three months" no-no's were, on the face of it, a lot more serious than others:

- **Go away for the weekend together.**
- **Break wind in front of him.**
- **Meet his parents.**
- **Introduce him to her parents.**
- **Burp in front of him.**
- **Wear slouchy clothes when he's around.**
- **Let him see her in big pants.**
- **Wear face cream in bed with him.**
- **Wear mismatched undies.**
- **Go make-up free.**

Meanwhile one in four women said they'd happily send a naughty text or a saucy selfie after the first date... What we're really afraid of is our partners seeing us as the undignified, imperfect people we sometimes are: we want to keep up a good image until we're sure we won't drive someone away. We want to be loved for our true selves – but sometimes we feel a need to present our polished selves before we risk revealing that our true self sometimes burps or wears big pants.

⊘ WANT TO SLOW THINGS DOWN?

If things are moving too fast, run yourself through this checklist:

1 **Why do I feel this way?** Am I not sure I want to be with this person at all? Or do I like them, but just don't feel ready for this much change in my life this soon? This is something you need to settle in your own mind right away, before you raise the subject with your date.

2 **What are the key issues?** Do I need more time to myself, or to spend with other people? Am I feeling territorial about my home? Are they talking like they're assuming a level of commitment I never promised? If you can identify exactly what's bothering you, you're likely to get a lot further.

3 **How do I think they'll take the news?** No one likes being told to back off when they're in love, but if you present it right, do you think your partner will accept it? Or will they refuse to respect your limits?

4 **What am I willing to do to compromise?** For instance: maybe I need more time to myself, but I can assure my partner that I do value our time together. Or: ideally I'd like my tiny apartment to myself, but I could clear a drawer for their stuff. Knowing what you're prepared to do in exchange for slowing down can help keep things positive. (If you're not willing to do anything, though, or your date won't compromise, are you sure you want to be in this relationship?)

KNOW YOUR BOUNDARIES
HOW TO KEEP YOUR LIMITS HEALTHY

Although we all have different ideas of the perfect balance in a relationship, we all want the right mix of closeness and independence. Where do we draw the line between intimate and inappropriate?

As we talk of "boundaries", it's useful to know exactly what we mean. Some boundaries are physical: people aren't allowed to touch you unless you allow it, and you get to determine which kinds of touch are acceptable and which aren't. Some are psychological and emotional: there are subjects that you'd rather not discuss, names you'd rather not be called, methods of persuasion you'd rather not be subjected to. Boundaries are how we preserve our physical and mental integrity: there are forms of contact and interaction that we'll accept with everyone, others that we'll accept with only a few close friends, others only with a romantic partner, and others with no one at all.

One sign of a potentially dangerous partner is their refusal to accept our boundaries (see pages 156–157), but negotiating them is an important part of even the healthiest relationship.

Where are your limits?

Think of your own boundaries in two ways. The first is as a measure of a potential partner's respect for you and compatibility with you: you want someone who both accepts your boundaries and communicates their own boundaries clearly – and has boundaries you can live with. If you hate talking about your childhood, say, a partner should respect that, but if they really aren't comfortable with someone whose childhood is a closed subject, you may just not work out.

It's all too easy to get into conflict about boundaries by mixing them up with issues of control. Boundaries put limits on other people's behaviour. When it comes to dating, it's crucial we choose someone who's prepared to respect those limits – not someone who exploits the concept and whose "boundaries" stop you doing things you have a right to do.

Drawing the line can sometimes be complicated, but the simplest line is this: if it's about doing something to you, it's a boundary; if it's about doing

MAKE YOURSELF HEARD

Communication is crucial, so make sure your tone isn't a distraction. If you can keep your approach constructive but assertive, you stand the best chance of success.

Passive	Assertive communication	Aggressive
Disrespecting oneself	Respecting both	Disrespecting the other

SETTING HEALTHY BOUNDARIES

What if you're not happy about something, or not willing to do something? Being clear about your own feelings is the best way to go – after all, your partner won't know (or can only guess) unless you tell them.

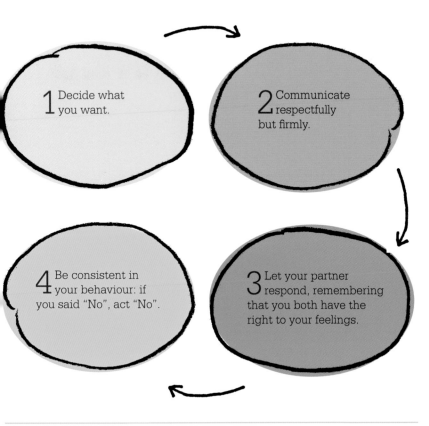

1 Decide what you want.

2 Communicate respectfully but firmly.

4 Be consistent in your behaviour: if you said "No", act "No".

3 Let your partner respond, remembering that you both have the right to your feelings.

> Boundaries show you treasure your life as your own best friend.
>
> **Jan Black**
> author of *Better Boundaries: Owning and Treasuring Your Life*

 KEEPING CLEAR ON YOURSELF

When we're deep in a relationship, we can sometimes lose track of what's "me" and what's my partner. A few tips to help you stay comfortably distinct:

✔ **Be self-aware.** Keep conscious of your own thoughts and opinions, including how they're like or unlike your partner's. Try to understand and accept what you're feeling, even if it's uncomfortable.

✔ **Assert yourself.** No need to be aggressive, but if you disagree, or want to do something, say so.

✔ **Respect your own interests.** If they're worthwhile to you, then they're worthwhile.

✔ **Set limits.** If something bothers you, bring it up and ask for change. You may have to compromise, but better to talk about it than push the feelings back down.

✔ **Look after yourself.** You need time to sleep, eat well, exercise, and have fun; no one can carry on without some self-care.

✔ **Be compassionate to yourself.** Everyone makes mistakes. Give yourself a break: your feelings matter even if you're not perfect.

something separate from you, such as chatting to an ex, it may be annoying, but it's not a boundary issue. "Don't tickle me" is laying down a boundary and should be accepted without argument; "Don't wear that stupid hat" is not a boundary and is subject to negotiation.

Am I still me?

The second crucial aspect of boundaries is maintaining your sense of self during a relationship: even a loving couple can find their identities blurring a little, and it helps refresh the relationship if you can keep

yourselves as two individuals. Minor disagreements and different interests needn't be a threat to the relationship; having someone around who sees things differently can provide an excellent reality check.

When it comes to finding love, the real question is this: which of your boundaries are non-negotiable, and which might you let down with the right person? This can be a great way to judge how comfortable you feel with a new partner. If they respect the former and you can picture them being allowed past the latter, you may be on to something wonderful.

NIPPING IT IN THE BUD

HOW TO STOP A SMALL PROBLEM TURNING INTO A BIG ONE

Your new partner keeps doing that thing that upsets or irritates you. You don't want to cause problems, and you haven't had your first row yet – but might you make things worse by staying quiet?

All of us can sometimes bottle things up in the early stages of a relationship – if it's new and precious, we dread breaking the spell. But it's inevitable that if you are going to stay in this relationship, you are going to have clashes.

Get it over with

How you navigate conflict will be crucial to your future happiness. Communication is key: you need to know whether it's safe to raise disagreements. Best find out while a problem is still small: if that comment they made this morning hurt your feelings, it's not a big deal for you to say, "Hey, I felt a bit upset today". If you store it up, saying "Hey, I felt a bit upset last month" will seem much worse, and the likely response – "You've been brooding on it all this time?" – won't get your first disagreement off on the right foot.

Consider a small problem as a dry run, and practise raising objections over something that bothers you but isn't too serious. That way, when something bigger comes up, you'll have a better idea of how to handle it.

No one likes to move out of the honeymoon, never-had-a-quarrel stage. But raising an issue doesn't necessarily mean having a quarrel,

---

 SNAPPISH OR SNACKISH?

Feeling annoyed with your partner? It could be your blood sugar. If you're irritable, you might be "hangry" (hungry and angry), so make sure you have a snack before you start a fight. The quickest way to fix your blood glucose levels is carbohydrates or sugar, so nibble on something carby or sweet and see if you feel better.

 GOOD OPENING LINES

Not sure how to bring it up? Try some of these:

> Listen, can we settle something? I'm kind of bothered by this and I'd like to move past it.

> I've been worrying about something and I'd like to sort it out with you – is that okay?

> You know yesterday? I'm sure you didn't mean it, but I've been feeling anxious about something.

> Hey, I'm feeling a bit upset – can we talk about it?

> There's something on my mind – is it okay if we clear the air?

and if your partner has upset you, the honeymoon is already over. It's time to move on to the "don't-have-any-problems-we-can't-handle" stage.

Admit it

Sometimes the issue isn't that your partner has upset you; it's that you've upset them. At this point, you may be terrified your partner will leave, or you may block them out to avoid a scene. But remember: if your partner is able to raise the issue constructively, that's a good sign. It means they want to resolve things with you: they want to do this relationship right.

The simplest solution is the best: apologies work. In 2014, a study in *PNAS* (*Proceedings of the National Academy of Sciences*) questioned 337 partners who'd had a serious fight: after a simple apology, they rated their partner more highly and felt more confident the relationship would last. It even made victims of crimes more likely to forgive the criminal.

Asking for and offering an apology is something anyone in a relationship has to do sometimes. Don't put it off: the quicker you do it, the quicker you can fix things and start to feel better. If you're not convinced, though, and feel anxious about apologizing, you might question whether you really want to be with a partner who wouldn't accept your apology or who'd turn it against you.

5 a day

Try a hug. The **ideal relationship has five cuddles a day,** according to 2,000 couples who took part in a UK survey.

THE PERFECT APOLOGY

The 2014 study in PNAS (see left) found that the most effective apologies had three components:

1 **Show and admit regret.** Say "I'm sorry" like you really are.

2 **Take responsibility.** None of that "I'm sorry you feel that way", or "I'm sorry if…". It's "I'm sorry I upset you" or nothing. If you did something wrong, own up to it and don't deflect. "Faux-apologies" just make you sound like a shady politician.

3 **Do something to make amends.** Sweep up the mess you made, book a nice evening together, offer a gift … the point is to do something that actively proves you want to help your partner feel better.

AND SO TO BED – OR NOT
PASSING THAT MAJOR THRESHOLD

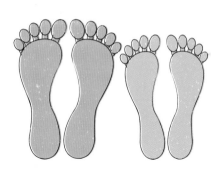

Few landmarks in a relationship are more major than the progress to sexual intimacy. When you go to bed is one of the most personal decisions you'll ever make. How do you decide when the time is right for you?

THINKING WITH YOUR HORMONES?

In studies of rats, virgin females injected with oxytocin – the hormone that is released by sex and propels bonding – snuggle up with other females' pups and care for them as if they were their own. When we bed someone, that hit of oxytocin may obscure how we felt about them before the sex.

29%

According to an ABC News poll in 2004, **29 per cent of Americans** have had **sex on a first date.**

The answer is going to depend on a lot of questions. Are you young and inexperienced, or mature and assured? Are you a free agent, or do you have children to consider? Are you feeling great and ready for anything, or do you need time to rebuild your confidence? Does your culture support non-marital sexual relationships, or do you need a serious commitment before you can even consider sex? All that's before you even consider your partner!

Watch your hormones

Before you jump into bed, take a little time to think. Sex isn't just about pleasure: it also releases hormones associated with bonding. Once you've had sex with someone, especially if the sex was good, you can find your feelings changing more than you expect: orgasms release oxytocin, known as the "cuddle hormone" – a potent chemical that makes us fall in love (see pages 154–155). That's great if you're with the right person, but it can also be useful if you're used to dating unsuitable people and you're trying to give a chance to someone nicer (see pages 130–131): a hit of oxytocin – and vasopressin, if you're a man – might get you over feeling only lukewarm and leave you blissfully bonded to someone suitable.

This does *not* mean that you have to sleep with someone you're not sure about, only that you may feel hotter for someone nice after you've gone to bed. It *does* mean be careful if you're dating someone unsuitable. They may be sexy, but sleeping with them won't get them "out of your system". Our hormones can play tricks on our emotions and judgement, so don't set yourself up for heartbreak.

Getting attached

Attachment styles can also lead us a merry dance when it comes to sex: see the chart opposite. Whatever your style, though, the best kind of long-term sexual relationship is one that's mutually satisfying, respectful, and affectionate, with a solid foundation of emotional connection as well as passion. Sex can be lovely in an emotionally strong relationship, so don't deny yourself the pleasure if you feel ready.

SEX AND ATTACHMENT

Whatever our attachment style (US population percentages are shown right), we carry it into the bedroom. Sex with emotional connection as well as passion is likely to come more naturally if you're secure than if you're anxious for reassurance or uncomfortable with intimacy. Do any of the issues below sound familiar?

50% SECURE   **20%** ANXIOUS   **25%** AVOIDANT

Attachment style	Fundamental fears	Motives	Potential risks
Secure	Not deeply afraid, but still vulnerable to normal fears of heartbreak.	■ Seeking closer connection and mutual pleasure. ■ The most likely to enjoy sex fully and have fun with it.	■ Staying with a sexually unsatisfying partner out of loyalty.
Anxious 	Frightened of rejection and hungry for acceptance. Anxiously attached women are more likely to be sexually assertive (when it's not necessarily what they want) or promiscuous. Anxiously attached men are more likely to be sexually reserved, if they think their female partners prefer this.	■ Liable to seek sex as a proof of acceptance – which undermines genuine intimacy and pleasure because it means the sex isn't really about sex. ■ Can take it personally if the sex doesn't go well that night, worrying it's a sign they'll be rejected soon. ■ Tend to worry that their partners don't love them if they aren't in the mood.	■ Often sexually unconfident. ■ Particularly vulnerable to sexual exploitation and coercion. ■ Most likely to accept risky practices such as unprotected sex. ■ Can jump to conclusions about the quality of the whole relationship based on a single sexual encounter, good or bad.
Avoidant 	Intimacy and closeness are scary in any context, including sex.	■ Can treat sex as "conquests", more to impress peers than get close to a lover. The most likely style to have many casual partners. ■ May try to substitute sex for emotional connection. ■ May prefer the safety of masturbation and/or pornography.	■ May avoid sex, or lose interest in a committed partner. Sex may not enrich the relationship even if the sex is good. ■ May find sex uncomfortable or embarrassing, lack skill in bed, or miss out on fun. ■ Can be exploitative. ■ Can be sexually active but lonely.

DRIVING YOU CRAZY
THE POWER OF THE UNRELIABLE

Does the amount you obsess about your dating partner reflect the amount of love you feel for them? Not necessarily: sometimes your biology can work against your best interests.

Have you ever been in a relationship where your partner often let you down, yet you couldn't stop thinking about them? Or have you ever met someone who was charming, attractive, and kind, and yet there wasn't the spark you'd felt with less devoted partners? Do you wish you could find someone exciting and nice, but suspect you can't have both? You're experiencing an "activated attachment system", and it happens to all of us.

Activated attachment systems
Whether it's a parent or a partner, we identify a central person as precious – and we need them to treat us as precious too. A 2011 study by Ethan Kross found that rejection hits the same parts of the brain that register physical pain: holding a very hot coffee cup and thinking about a recent break-up lit up the same areas on an fMRI scan. Rejection literally "hurts". When we feel that pain, we can't take it: our attachment system

"activates", pushing us to find ways to feel soothed and safe again. If we're secure, we can soothe ourselves as well as draw comfort from others. Avoidant people "deactivate", pulling away from people and trying to calm down independently. Anxious people "hyperactivate", looking to their precious person for reassurance and unable to calm down without it.

If we get the reassurance we need, our brain rewards us with oxytocin, the "cuddle hormone", and dopamine – a chemical that activates the same neural circuits as cocaine and heroin. With each new upset, we chase the "hit" we need, and the reassurance. If you're an anxious person dating an avoidant partner, they probably won't want to give it to you. Their self-

THE ANXIOUS-AVOIDANT VICIOUS CIRCLE
Anxious people are most worried about abandonment and react by pushing for reassurance. Avoidant people are most worried about being emotionally overwhelmed and react by pushing for space. The result can be a never-ending cycle of mutual misunderstanding and stress.

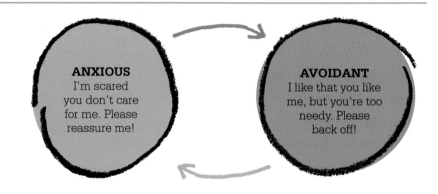

ANXIOUS
I'm scared you don't care for me. Please reassure me!

AVOIDANT
I like that you like me, but you're too needy. Please back off!

soothing mechanism depends on shutting other people out. If the avoidant partner relents and gives some reassurance, the relief can lead to an oxytocin/dopamine rush. If the relationship becomes a dizzying rollercoaster of highs and lows, your brain starts to crave those highs, since it's the closest you get to love.

Needing the high

If you're an anxious person who's used to dating avoidants, be aware. Because the lows are so intense, the highs feel amazing: this, thinks your brain, must be what passion feels like. Except it's not passionate love – it's passionate relief.

There are two risks here. One, that you'll stay in an unhappy relationship because the highs are so compelling. Two, that if you meet someone new, you may find them unexciting (see pages 130–131) because they don't produce the highs – but that's only because they don't produce the lows. With a secure person, the rush may be gentler, but the supply is steadier. Love will feel different, but better.

🔍 **CONNECTION AS A PAINKILLER**

If rejection is painful, love is a pretty good analgesic. A 2006 study led by James Coan at the University of Virginia gave small electric shocks to 16 women who described themselves as happily married. If they got the shock by themselves, they reported it as very painful. If they got it while holding a stranger's hand, they reported it as fairly painful. But if they got to hold their husband's hand, they said it was only uncomfortable. A steady connection with someone can spare you pain as well.

WHO WINS?

A full-on anxious/avoidant clash makes both partners unhappy even if they really do love each other – but it tends to be the avoidant partner who gets more of their way. It's simply easier to say "No" than it is to force someone to reassure you. The two can end in diametrically opposite places, one needing more, the other less:

ANXIOUS

I feel upset. I need some love.

Oh, no, you're pulling away! Please reassure me you still love me.

Am I too needy? Maybe I'm just unlovable. Please tell me I'm not unloveable!

Now you're pulling away even more! I feel awful.

This relationship must be in serious trouble. I can't bear the thought of losing you.

AVOIDANT

My partner's upset? This is stressful – I don't need this.

Oh boy, I can't handle this drama. I need some space.

Stop hassling me! What's wrong with you?!

Maybe this isn't worth it. At least if I'm single I'll have some peace.

I've had it. Let's just break up.

Once a conflict reaches this point, the avoidant is more comfortable saying "My way or the highway", and there's not much an anxious partner can do but accept one or the other. The chance for real intimacy is lost, and neither side benefits – though the avoidant person may be less aware of this than the anxious one.

RELUCTANT FIRE
THE POWER OF EXCITEMENT

Your potential new partner is nice, interesting, fun … everything you want, except they don't excite you. If you could just get a spark going, everything would be perfect. Can you make yourself fall in love?

If you fall for someone without even trying, then it's reasonable to assume that you have a natural spark. But you may well encounter a person who seems right for you but just doesn't get your blood racing. Likeable companions don't come along every day, so it's a big decision: do you "settle", do you turn them down and keep looking (at the risk of not finding anyone as nice), or is there a third option?

Get your head straight
First ask yourself this: is your lack of butterflies really a lack of chemistry, or is your past getting you confused? If you're in the habit of dating people who mess you around, sometimes you start conflating attraction with anxiety (see pages 148–149): make sure that's not your problem before you make any big decisions.

On the other hand, it may be that this person is not your type. If you physically can't bear them, it's probably best to call it quits – but if you aren't repelled, just not very attracted, you can help to make love happen, or at least give it a nudge…

Check the label
According to American psychologists Elaine Hatfield and Ellen Berscheid, what they call the "two-factor theory of love" comes into play here: the two factors are arousal and labels.

Put simply, we associate love with excitement – and sometimes we can also reverse the two, associating excitement with love. If we've just survived a car crash or won an award, the next person we meet will stand a much better chance of attracting us: our hearts are pumping and our hands are shaking, and on some level our brains can assume that this person is the cause. We don't like to be unclear on why we're feeling what we're feeling, so we look for explanations – and sometimes we get the explanation

THE MISATTRIBUTION OF AROUSAL

We may think we know our feelings, but the physical sensations of fear, excitement, and desire are almost identical. Sometimes we feel the sensations first, then attribute them to whichever emotion seems likeliest in the circumstances.

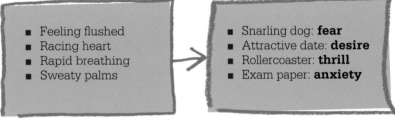

- Feeling flushed
- Racing heart
- Rapid breathing
- Sweaty palms

Physiological arousal

- Snarling dog: **fear**
- Attractive date: **desire**
- Rollercoaster: **thrill**
- Exam paper: **anxiety**

Labelling

wrong, through misattribution of arousal. Here's the twist: if we tell ourselves we're excited because this person is gorgeous, the subsequent excitement probably will be partly caused by this person.

Playing with fire?

If the two-factor theory of love works on us, then by doing something particularly thrilling on a date (see below), we might find ourselves growing more attracted. The key is to do it for the right reasons. Lighting a reluctant fire for someone just because they're there, because they seem "suitable", or because you haven't met anyone else, will only store up trouble. Before you start flooding your system with adrenalin, go on a couple of dates to see if you actually enjoy this person's company. You deserve someone who makes you happy, and only you can be the judge of whether this person might do that – but if they might, give adrenalin a chance and you could find yourself more attracted than you supposed.

> Trapeze artists must have complicated and compelling love lives.
>
> **David McRaney**
> Journalist and blogger, on the misattribution of arousal

 ## NEED TO GET EXCITED?

To light a reluctant fire, try arousing some of these emotions for your date:

- ✔ **Fear.** Horror movies are popular with courting couples. If you're more of a physical daredevil, then rollercoasters, parachuting, and extreme sports are another option – at least you'll have a fun date, even if it doesn't turn into romance.

- ✔ **Anger.** Do you and your date share a common outrage at some injustice in society? Go on a march or get involved in some activism. If you can get angry together, you may see each other through new eyes.

- ✔ **Urgency.** Set strict deadlines for the end of a date so you have to enjoy every minute as the final hour approaches. (Probably best not to tell your date you're doing this one.)

- ✔ **Drama.** Romantic music and films are notorious for getting us in the mood. If you both like opera or weepies, pick something grandiose and see if you can share a good sob.

- ✔ **Sexual arousal.** Look through a few naughty pictures or read a bit of erotic fiction before the date; some mild sexual frustration might make your date look all the hotter.

THE TORMENTS OF LOVE

If you and your date get to the point of physical intimacy, you might consider a little role-play to spice things up. Stony Brook psychologist Arthur Aron found that some fictional drama could make a real difference. When he cast male student volunteers as soldiers being "tortured" for information by a female research assistant, they became increasingly attracted to their "interrogator". You needn't go that far if it's not to your taste. But if you do decide to get sexual, a little bit of fantasy can heighten the excitement – just make sure your partner is willing to take part.

ROMANTIC LOVE IS ONE OF THE MOST ADDICTIVE SUBSTANCES ON EARTH

HELEN FISHER, ANTHROPOLOGIST AND RESEARCH PROFESSOR, RUTGERS UNIVERSITY

SPOTTING REAL DANGER
WARNING SIGNS OF AN ABUSER

Some people always "hurt the ones they love", but it usually takes a while for the victim – and others – to see it. The sooner the better, though, so how can you see abuse coming before it gets really bad?

Abuse is often invisible. Victims struggle with mixed messages if others see their partner as a great person – the victim may agree, in many ways, and yet still feel emotionally damaged by their controlling behaviour. If you're in this situation, pay attention to your emotions. Spotting an abuser early can be a matter of life or death: of the women murdered by partners, around three-quarters are killed while trying to leave. The sooner you realize someone is dangerous, the less they have invested in the relationship and the more likely they are to let go. It's also easier for you to leave, before they wear down your resistance.

What makes someone abusive? Some – but not all – abusers had painful childhoods, but many people with a bad start make respectful and compassionate partners. Whatever the cause, the essence of an abuser is this: they feel entitled to a partner who never crosses or displeases them, and justified in using intimidation,

bullying, and/or manipulation when their actual partner (inevitably) does something they don't like.

No one is abusive all the time – in fact, the nice periods are part of the abusive cycle. Nor are all abusers physically violent – some never even shout, but issue a steady stream of hurtful and degrading remarks.

When you're with someone new, watch out for the following signs:

- **They're controlling.** Control is central to abuse, and a lot of abuse is punishment for resisting control. Do you get a say in the plans? Do they have an image they insist you live up to? Do you get to say no?
- **They're possessive.** It feels flattering to be wanted, but do they act as if they own you? Do they see your interests outside the relationship as a positive or a threat? Are they trustful or jealous?
- **They rush things.** Abusers often (though not always) press for early commitment, talking of love, moving in, and marriage before they really know you. They may be more in love with a fantasy than the real you – and may turn nasty if you deviate from that fantasy.
- **They try to isolate you.** An abuser wants their partner to think and care about nothing but them.

15%

The National Crime Victimization Survey reports that in 2011, **violence from intimate partners (male and female)** accounted for almost **15 per cent of all violent crime in the USA.**

30%

Four per cent of women reported being **slapped or shoved** by an intimate partner during 2010 in the USA; **30 per cent** have been slapped or shoved by a partner **at some point in their lives.**

JUST CAN'T WIN

A potential stepmother walks a fine line. If she's cautious, children may see her as cold and mean – but as researchers Larry Ganong and Marilyn Coleman at the University of Missouri found in 2011, children may reject a warm and sympathetic stepmother. Her kindness draws them to her, which makes the children feel disloyal to their own mother, so they push her away. Patience rather than extra effort is best – plus, if at all possible, their mother saying, "It's okay to like so-and-so, I know it doesn't mean you love me less."

♥ DIVIDED LOYALTIES

When your loyalties are divided between different "camps", there are several areas that create worry, for the new partner and the children. It's probably best to clarify which are the major concerns in your relationship – it will depend partly on the age of your children and partly on your situation – so that you can head off worries early.

- **Love:** Do I matter to you as much as your children / partner?
- **Attention:** Are you more interested in your children / partner than me?
- **Empathy:** If one of us acts badly, who gets forgiven and who gets told to forgive?
- **Resources:** How are we / you going to allocate money and time?
- **Role:** Am I still your baby? Am I still the smart one / pretty one / mature one?
- **Status:** Who matters most now? Who rules the roost? Who'll get their way? You / your partner / your kids?
- **Loyalty:** Who should be loyal to whom, and how do I show my allegiance?

- **Get your partner on board** with the idea of divided authority. It's not fair to ask you to be the tough one while the kids' actual parent plays best buddy. "Contributive authority" enables and provides good things; "corrective authority" disciplines and guides. Children need both. If you have to divide it up, make the parent corrective and the partner contributive, so the partner's "bad guy" status starts to dissipate.

Keep a separate space

Remember the relationship is about the two of you as well as the whole family. If the children start conflicts, don't refight them when you're alone – and take time out as a couple so that there's more to the relationship than worrying about the family.

Exactly how well a "blended family" will work is hard to predict and hard to control. Keep the expectations low and the standards of courtesy high: a couple who can survive introducing the children to each other can survive pretty much anything.

44%

In the USA in 2009, an online dating agency called Match.com reported that **44 per cent** of its members **had children.**

42%

In a 2011 study, the Pew Research Center reports that **42 per cent of American adults** have at least **one step-relative,** rising to **52 per cent** in the **under-30s**.

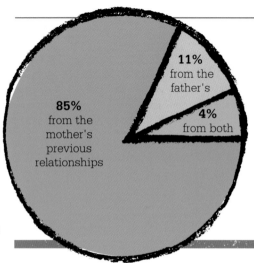

85% from the mother's previous relationships

11% from the father's

4% from both

UK STEPFAMILIES

In 2011, Britain's ONS (Office for National Statistics) estimated that 11 per cent of UK couples with dependent children were stepfamilies. Of these 544,000 families, 4 per cent included stepchildren from both partners' previous relationships, 11 per cent from the father's previous relationships, and 85 per cent from the mother's.

OVERLAPPING YOUR CIRCLES
MEETING EACH OTHER'S FRIENDS

If you're building a relationship, you're going to meet each other's other favourite people. You hope they'll be lovely, and welcome you with open arms. If not, does it make any difference whether you get on with them?

It's sensible to want your partner's friends to be supportive. Your social networks can make a big difference to romantic relationships – not just in their attitude towards your relationship, but towards romance in general. A study published in 2002 in the *North American Journal of Psychology* found that the less supportive their friends and family were, the more likely a partner was to be unfaithful. If their best pals all talk about cheating as though it's funny or inevitable, you aren't being too touchy if you feel worried.

> Social networks can make a big difference to relationships – not just in their attitude to your relationship but towards romance in general.

Why does it matter?

There are two main reasons why social support makes a difference. The more serious is that unsupportive companions can undermine you. A 2010 study by psychologists at the Mississippi State University found that unsupportive friends were more prone to "internal attributions" than "external attributions" for relationship problems – that is, they were more likely to write off their friend's partner with, "He's just a loser", or "You and she just aren't right together", than something less blaming, like, "Well, you're both under a lot of job stress right now" – and that partners were likely to listen to these sweeping judgements, especially if the social group was peers rather than family.

WHO'S MOST SUSCEPTIBLE?

As with so many aspects of relationships, someone's attachment style can make a big difference in how they deal with the views of family and friends. At Mississippi State University in 2010, a study in social networks found the following patterns:

Attachment style	Influence of family	Influence of friends
Secure	Particularly likely to be influenced	Somewhat likely to be influenced
Anxious	Unlikely to be influenced	Very likely to be influenced
Avoidant	Seldom influenced	Seldom influenced

The attachment style of your partner, therefore, may mean that lack of support in some quarters may not affect you: avoidant people tend not to listen to anyone (though they can be tricky partners in other ways), while anxious people tend to listen less to parents and more to friends.

The less drastic issue is that you're probably going to be spending a lot of time around your new partner's friends. If this is a problem for you, decide why you don't like them: are they just not your sort of people, or do they make you feel disrespected? If it's the former, it's not disastrous: you can negotiate a balance between separate social lives and the odd boring group event. If it's the latter, does your partner realize you feel disrespected? How they support you is what matters, not their friends.

If it goes wrong

If you just don't like your partner's friends, it can be worrying, especially if you're of the anxious attachment style, but here are three key points:

- **The friends were there before you,** but that doesn't mean they were chosen over you. Time can change priorities.

- **If the friendships give your partner something you don't,** that's not a threat to you: no one can be everything to everybody.
- **If your partner clearly enjoys being with their friends,** especially if they're extroverted (see pages 36–37), this doesn't mean they want to get away from you.

On the other hand, suppose your partner doesn't like your friends:

- **You and your friends aren't identical,** so not liking them isn't a criticism of you.
- **You already know what's good about your friends.** Your partner doesn't have to validate that.
- **Are you happy with your partner in general?** Then you're fine. They don't have to enjoy everything you do, or the company of everyone you know.

FRIENDS WITH AN EX?

Be honest about it: the longer you leave it a secret, the more it'll seem a big deal. You may need to reassure your partner that there's nothing in it, but see that as a way to check your new relationship is healthy. If nothing you say will convince them that an old flame is now just a friend, you should take that seriously: a possessive partner can be wearing at best, dangerous at worst (see pages 156–157). On the other hand, showing a little concern is a sign that your partner sees you as a person lots of people would be attracted to. That's a compliment: if your partner is prepared to trust you once you make it clear that you only have eyes for them now, then they're showing they think you're a catch.

BUT I MISS YOU SO

HOW MUCH TIME TOGETHER IS RIGHT?

Even long-established couples can feel that they're spending too much or too little time together, so if you feel that in the early days, it's not a disaster. What's the best way to work out a compromise?

> How about we make Tuesdays just the two of us?

When it comes to how much time to spend together, everybody has their idea of perfect bliss. It can vary depending on where you are in the relationship and what else is going on in your life – but what if you can't agree on how much time you should be spending in each other's company?

There may be several different explanations behind the problem, and the solution will vary according to each. The following scenarios are far from exhaustive, but whatever the dynamics of your relationship, healthy communication offers a way to both understand your particular dilemma and find a way out of it.

 ARE YOU AVOIDING ME?

The problem:
People with an avoidant attachment style start to feel jittery or stifled if they spend "too much" time in their partner's company. Conscious fears of being controlled and frustrated – and unconscious fears of being neglected or abandoned – play on their minds, and the partner starts to look like a threat.

The result:
Avoidant people can, literally, start to avoid their partner. If you aren't living together yet, this is fairly easy to do: avoidants are always "too busy" or they have social engagements that they simply have to go to – or they invite their partner along but the events are so crowded that you don't really spend time together.

> Can I take a few hours of alone time so I can focus on you when I get back?

What not to do:
If this turns into a serious conflict and the avoidant isn't very much in love with their partner – or even, sometimes, if they are – they can end up giving an ultimatum or ending the relationship.

A good solution:
✔ If you're the avoidant, schedule some regular "me time", where you can have your space and relax.

✔ Schedule some regular "us time", when you commit to giving your partner your full attention.

✔ **Make sure there's a fair balance** of these in every week. Above all, tell your partner why you're doing this. "Me time" is less worrying for them if they know it's partly your way of preparing for "us time".

 INTROVERT OR
EXTROVERT?

The problem:
Sometimes introverts like to be alone, which can make a partner feel shut out. They also love quiet time with their partner. Extroverts love sociable events: too much quiet, and they feel cooped up; too much of the other, and the introvert feels there's never any peace. Even two extroverts may have different needs.

The result:
An introvert can often feel hurt if a more extroverted partner counts going to parties together as "us time". While the avoidant uses other people to block their connection, extroverts use other people to charge up the connection: the feeling is not relief that other people are acting as buffers, but pleasure that the two of you are partying together.

What not to do:
Each partner can pressure the other into doing things their way, but without good communication, the extrovert feels guilty for dragging the introvert around and the introvert feels guilty for trapping the extrovert at home.

A good solution:
✔ Each partner makes clear how their preferred activity helps them feel close to their partner, so you both see how it's helping the relationship.

✔ The couple agrees a minimum amount of "in" and "out" time per week. This shouldn't be too inflexible – life's not that predictable – but provision should be made for each person's needs.

✔ The couple may like to identify a particular time to spend apart charging up their batteries, and then have a proper night in together.

 QUALITY OR
QUANTITY?

The problem:
Not everyone has the same definition of "time together". Is it time together if you're both in the house but doing your own thing? Or you're watching TV and not talking? Or you're doing the chores?

The result:
If there's a difference of expectations, each partner can feel the other is being unfair. The person who feels none of the time you've spent together "counts" now feels short-changed. The person who thinks it *was* all time together now feels their partner is impossible to satisfy. Each may really want time with the other but be bewildered and possibly offended by their partner's attitude.

What not to do:
You argue. You haggle. You accuse. You waste what time you do have together in acrimonious disputes.

A good solution:
✔ Distinguish between time together and "active engagement". A healthy relationship has both, but active engagement means talking with each other, paying close attention to the other's reactions, and doing something you both enjoy.

✔ Remember that it's not wrong to find more passive time together fulfilling as well. Some people draw a primal satisfaction from just being near their partner, and that's a sign of affection.

> I love our home movie nights – let's make some popcorn.

 FIND TIME
OR MAKE TIME

The problem:
Some of us are very, very busy. We may want romance, but there never seems to be a moment to do it justice.

The result:
Even if we've met someone we like, things keep coming up. The relationship just isn't happening because there isn't enough space for it.

> Crisis at work right now, but I'll make it up to you, I promise!

What not to do:
The relationship withers and dies simply because no one watered it. Alternatively, it becomes more of a convenient arrangement than real closeness, and the less-busy partner feels neglected and bad about themselves.

A good solution:
✔ Be honest with yourself. If you're in a temporary emergency, okay, you may not have a minute – but don't sit back and wait for it to resolve itself: get out your diaries and get on that schedule. Make time. It might be tucked into the corners, but a corner is better than nothing.

✔ If you wanted to have a proper, fancy dinner to make up for all the cancelled dates, but your boss has just demanded another all-nighter, you could still meet for a sandwich. Making an obvious effort to find the time to see your partner now makes better amends than any bouquet or bottle of wine later.

✔ Work towards a conclusion. If there is a crisis at work, it'll come to an end at some point. Even if you don't know when the end will be, make it clear to your partner that once it arrives, you'll make up for lost time.

SO ARE WE A COUPLE NOW?

THE TRANSITION TO COMMITMENT

There comes a point in every serious relationship when the initial thrilling uncertainty – or painful anxiety, depending on your disposition – has to end. How do you settle that you're going from "dating" to "item"?

Talking about love can be a major part of commitment (see pages 170–171), but it's not the only transition: people can start falling in love without being officially committed, and can also commit without talking about love – after all, in some cultures people expect love to come after marriage, and in others people may be very sincerely committed but just undemonstrative in their speech.

Let's talk about it

Three topics you may need to cover:

1 **Exclusivity**
When and whether you can date multiple people varies widely (see pages 132–133), but long term it's risky to make assumptions. If you're both naturally monogamous people, then it probably won't be a long conversation, but if there's any uncertainty, it's best to be clear that you're ready to stop dating other people to make this an exclusive commitment – and find out whether your partner is as well.

6-8

American couples say it takes **six to eight dates** before they are willing to enter into **an exclusive relationship**, according to dating author Paul F. Davis.

2 Status

How do you refer to each other? It's a small verbal change, but a big social one, when you start calling someone your boyfriend, girlfriend, or partner. These words announce to the world that you and this person have stopped considering each other as prospects and are now considering each other as chosen companions – perhaps for ever, perhaps not, but certainly for now.

There are two popular ways to tackle this: either you talk openly with each other about whether you can use those words, or you do it by experiment: call someone your boyfriend/girlfriend/partner in their hearing – in private, not public – and see if they object or smile.

The try-it-and-see route is more risky if you're not sure they're keen, as they may have to either accept more than they're comfortable with or embarrass you with a contradiction. Talking about it first can seem less spontaneous, more tentative, but it is clear about consent. Which route works for you is going to depend on the dynamic between you. Either way, first ask yourself whether the label you want is a realistic fit with how you are together, before you try to move to the next level of intimacy.

> Girlfriend? Lady friend? Partner? Which sounds right?

3 Roles

If you're still just dating and have yet to move in, buy a puppy, and open a joint bank account, it can seem premature to talk about issues such as household chores, bread-winning, and work-life balance. But you can fall into a role early on in a relationship and then find yourself stuck with it – and changing things once routines have built around them will be more of a strain. Smaller issues – who pays for meals out, who makes whose bed, who shops for whose dad's birthday – can be indicators of expectations, both yours and your partner's. You might like to raise all this as a general point about how it worked in past relationships or in your family while you were growing up, and how you both feel about it now. It's smart to get those expectations clear sooner rather than later; letting resentment build up helps no one.

It can take a bit of courage to get past these three transitions, but in a good relationship, they'll feel one of two ways: exciting, because there's this wonderful new person in your life, or relaxing, because it feels safe and natural. Or perhaps both at once!

🔍 STEP BY STEP

A classic experiment in 1966 by psychologists J.L. Freedman and S.C. Fraser shows the advantages of "foot-in-the-door" baby steps in commitment. Volunteers were asked to do the researchers either a large favour or a small favour followed by a request for the large one. The group asked for a small favour was almost twice as likely to agree to the big one: it seems that doing something small for someone makes you feel willing to do more later. If you're eager to settle down, start small – leave a toothbrush at each other's place, or have a regular sleepover night – before you make any bigger proposals.

> I'd like to tell my Dad we're an item – is that okay?

🔍 THE RULE OF COMMITMENT

There's a good reason these issues are best discussed between the two of you before you go public. The "Rule of Commitment" is one that sales people exploit a lot: once you've publicly said that you'll do something, you feel serious pressure to go through with it even if you aren't sure you want to. The hardsell may work in marketing, but in a relationship, you still have to deal with each other after the "sell" is finished, so check with each other before you announce anything.

Commitment phobia

This term was coined by self-help author Steven Carter in his 1987 bestseller *Men Who Can't Love*. Modern psychologists often argue that it is our old friend, avoidant attachment. If you or your partner feel an irrational panic at the thought of making things official, check your attachment style on pages 16–21.

RELATIONSHIPS ARE NOT JUST ABOUT TOGETHERNESS AND CONNECTION. THEY'RE ALSO ABOUT SPACES OF SEPARATENESS

LINDA AND CHARLIE BLOOM, RELATIONSHIP THERAPISTS

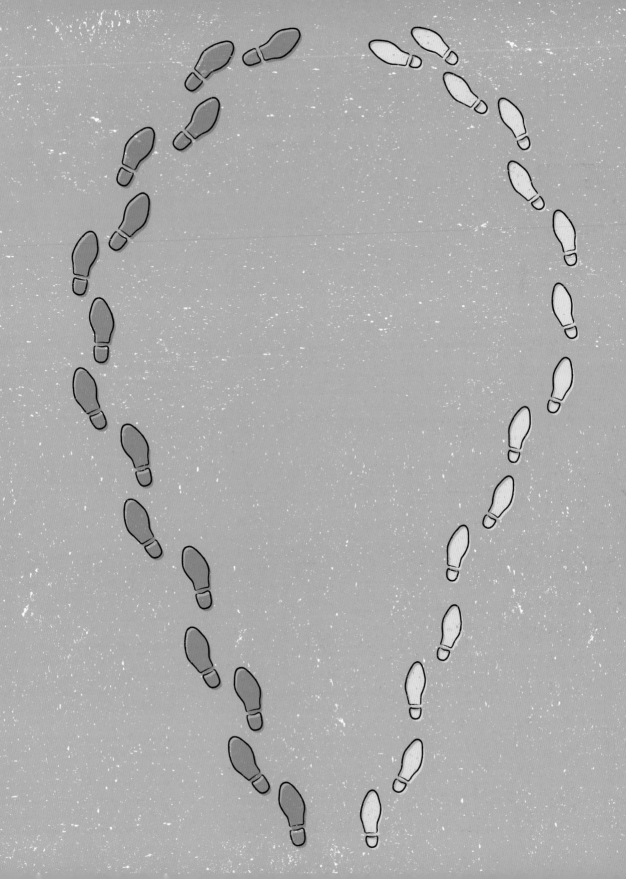

HERE'S YOUR KEY

MOVING IN TOGETHER

One minute you're leaving a spare toothbrush at your partner's place, and the next you're talking about moving in. Is that a step towards commitment – and eventually marriage, perhaps – or just a new normal?

Making the move from regular sleepovers to sharing your space is one of the big transitions of a relationship. We all have our worries about it... Will this trigger a commitment panic? What if he/she hates all my daily habits? What if we change our minds? Might we feel trapped in the relationship? Is living together the only path to happiness?

Am I ready?

A major consideration for living together is maturity: are you old enough to assume you won't grow apart? In the US, a 2014 study by the Council on Contemporary Families investigated the debate whether cohabiting before marriage increased or decreased the chances of divorce if you later marry, and came to a simple conclusion: what matters is the age at which you commit, whether by marrying or by moving in together. Younger people are less likely to pick a suitable long-term partner, or else more likely to change a lot after the relationship begins. Couples who

 CHANGING SOCIAL MORES

Beginning in the 1970s and up to the 2000s, there have been nearly a dozen serious studies that suggest couples living together before marrying were more likely to divorce than couples who went straight from dating to marriage. That may have changed now, thanks to changing social mores. You had to be more unconventional to cohabit in 1970 than you do today, and a free-spirited person has always been more likely to up and go than to stick it out if they aren't happy.

ENDING A SHORT RELATIONSHIP

Most of us don't like to disappoint people, so when we don't want to carry on dating someone, the temptation is to drop out of touch and hope they'll take the hint. But that's not really fair: it's more respectful to let them know there's no point waiting around for you. Some people can be persistent, though, so how do you minimize the chances of them pestering you?

Rule	Reason	Wrong	Right
Be clear	"Breaking it gently" can be confusing if you're so gentle that it doesn't sound like a proper rejection, especially if they're the type to cling to a false hope. You need to say directly that you don't want to carry on seeing this person.	"I'm just not in a good place right now."	"I've been thinking about us, and I need to let you know that I don't want to carry on seeing you."
Keep to the point	Why you don't want to date them isn't the issue: the issue is that you don't. If they want an explanation, don't go into details: the more reasons you give, the more opportunities they have to argue or promise to change.	"That thing you do really bothers me."	"I just don't see myself with you, and I don't think I ever will."
Be polite	Not only is being polite the right thing to do, but it will save you trouble in the long run: don't do anything that will allow them to justify chasing you for an apology or for "closure".	"You're an awful person, so why would I want to be with you?"	"I'm sorry if this isn't what you want to hear, but I've made up my mind."
Don't over-praise	Compliments may cushion the blow, but too many cushions and they may think that you're not sure of your own feelings and that you might just need more convincing.	"You're really smart and nice and attractive, and I'm sure you'd make a great partner."	"You're a great person, just not for me."
Only say no once	Once you've said no, you've said all you have to say. Don't return subsequent e-mails or phone calls. Silence is the clearest rejection of all: it tells a pushy suitor that your refusal is so firm that you're not even going to waste time repeating it.	"Would you please stop contacting me? I've already said no."	Say nothing and get on with your life.

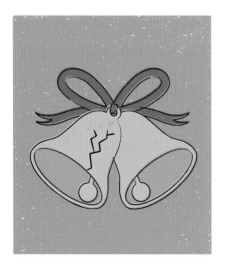

DO YOU OR DON'T YOU?

TIME TO TALK ABOUT MARRIAGE

The relationship looks pretty solid, and people are starting to hint at wedding bells. One of you is eager, but the other doesn't want to marry. If that sounds familiar, it's time for some serious communication.

WANT TO GET MARRIED?

Of all the occasions for hurt feelings and crossed wires, few can compare to a relationship where one partner wants to get married and the other doesn't. It's time to ask: what does marriage mean to you, and what does your partner need to understand?

? IT'S PROOF OF COMMITMENT

- **Reason:** to you, marriage is the final stage in a natural process, and refusing to take that step is refusing to show you're serious.

- **This can be a problem if:** you're expecting marriage to solve or prevent problems – after all, marriage is not a magic bullet.

- **This can be okay if:** you know that the relationship matters more than the label for it – but you do like the label, too.

? IT'S ROMANTIC

- **Reason:** you've always dreamed of a wedding and a ring, and it just feels too sad to give that dream up.

- **This can be a problem if:** your dream is more about the accessories than the actual person.

- **This can be okay if:** you really do care most about your partner – the romance of getting and being married is something you want to share with them.

? IT'S MORALLY RIGHT

- **Reason:** for religious or other reasons, you believe that marriage is the bedrock of family and society and that a respectable couple ought to be married.

- **This can be a problem if:** you're too dogmatic or judgmental about this, or you're more interested in marriage as a concept than in this particular person. It's also a problem if you have a serious clash of values with your partner.

- **This can be okay if:** your partner shares or at least respects your values, and is prepared for some serious discussion with you.

{ Remind yourselves that the most important commitment is to each other's wellbeing. }

2,118,000

US records show that more than **2.1 million marriages took place in 2011**. In the UK, around 248,000 marriages took place that year.

 54%
A 2013 gallup poll shows **more than half** of all Americans **are married.** In the UK, 47 per cent of the population is married.

Around **one in five** Americans has never married, but **would like to marry some day.** **21%**

5% One in 20 Americans has never married and **does not want to marry.**

The rest were once but are no longer married, or choose not to give their marital status. **20%**

DON'T WANT TO GET MARRIED?

It's perfectly possible to have a happy relationship without marriage as long as both of you are comfortable with that. The only "wrong" decision is to leave your reasons unexplored – so communicate as much as possible and remind yourselves that the most important commitment is to each other's wellbeing.

? IT'S A WASTE OF MONEY

- **Reason:** weddings are expensive – if you eloped and married on the cheap, your family would be hurt, and you just don't see the point of blowing all that money on one day.

- **This can be a problem if:** money isn't the real reason – you can get married on a limited budget – but you just don't want to marry this person. It's also a problem if you guilt-trip your partner for wanting it.

- **This can be okay if:** you feel so committed to your partner that you really do just think there's no point spending money to prove it.

? IT'S A RECIPE FOR DISASTER

- **Reason:** you saw your parents or other loved ones trapped in a terrible marriage. While you may love your partner very much and have no particular expectations of things going bad, marriage means closing the emergency exit, and you don't feel that would be safe for either of you.

- **This can be a problem if:** you're afraid of any kind of commitment to a full relationship. Things can go wrong between unmarried couples too, though, and if you're scared of being with anyone on a really serious basis, then you probably need to do some work on your fears, perhaps even in therapy. Not all relationships end badly.

- **This can be okay if:** you're content with being committed and are prepared to let your partner know that you're in it for the long haul – it's just the M-word that makes you nervous. You may need to prove your commitment in other ways, but if you can do that, the issue may be negotiable.

? IT'S A MATTER OF PRINCIPLE

- **Reason:** you think that marriage is wrong. You don't like the state or religion getting involved in your love life; you think it's unfair that marriage gives special status to couples or (in many countries) to heterosexuals; you think it's an outdated tradition.

- **This can be a problem if:** your "principle" is actually an excuse and you just don't want to marry this particular person, or you don't like the idea of being "tied down". (The latter is probably indicative of an avoidant attachment style.)

- **This can be okay if:** you're serious about love and relationships, it's just that you really don't see why marriage is necessary. If it's truly important to your partner, though, this is one of those occasions where you might want to consider some sort of compromise, or at least do something else to prove your commitment.

POPPING THE QUESTION
THE ART OF THE PROPOSAL

This is it: this person is the one for you, your lifelong partner, and you're sure of it. If you're dreaming of getting married, can the way you propose make a difference to your chances of a yes or a no?

arriage proposals can be daunting. Exactly how to go about it varies from culture to culture: for some people, it's either a courtesy or a necessity to ask the girl's parents before asking the girl, while other women expect to be the first person in the family to hear about the engagement, not the last. Some find public proposals endearing, while others cringe at the thought. How to navigate all this?

Expectations
First ask yourself this: what sort of proposal seems to be popular in your social setting? What is your beloved's idea of a nice proposal? You might hazard a guess based on their favourite Hollywood romance, but you're likely to get a more realistic idea from looking at what their friends do.

This may be particularly true if you're a man thinking of proposing to your girlfriend: women generally talk to each other a lot, and a particularly lovely (or awful) proposal story will undoubtedly go the rounds. Your friends, though, may feel a little put out if you propose extra beautifully to your girl: they may be happy for you, but they're also aware that if they want to propose, you've just raised the standard they'll have to meet.

On the other hand, if you're a woman thinking of proposing to your boyfriend, you may find yourself at an advantage – even if you don't propose at midnight in a gondola, the fact that you're doing the asking puts you ahead of most other women. If he strongly objects to the role reversal, though, it may be time to reconsider: as a woman who is open to pushing the boundaries of gender politics, do you really want to marry someone who is that much more conservative about such things?

Do you have the ring?

In an ideal world, a sensible person will say yes or no to a proposal based on their long-term hopes, not on the proposal itself. Alarmingly, though, according to one survey in 2010, 28 per cent of American women said they'd turn down a proposal if the ring wasn't right, but 45 per cent of American men said they'd done no research before buying the ring. This is hardly good news for the couples.

Turning down a great guy (or girl) because they've bought the wrong ring is pretty silly – that's a time for open dialogue, specifically that you'd like a different ring but not a different partner. It's not an entirely frivolous reaction, though: if you tend not to communicate much as a couple, it's easy to look to a ring to "speak" for you. Your partner might just have a limited budget or no eye for jewellery, but a ring thoughtlessly chosen doesn't send a good signal: you will probably be wearing it for the rest of your life, and a little consideration for your taste is a sign they'll consider your feelings.

Of course, rings are optional and an increasing number of couples decide to save the money, but the most important thing about a ring is that, like everything else in life, it can't be a substitute for communication.

Proposing marriage is one of those times you simply have to take a gamble, but you can at least take an informed gamble. Try to study up your beloved's expectations, tastes, and preferences, and above all, try to have as good an understanding of each other as possible in advance. That way, a proposal can be a romantic gesture without having to be a complete leap in the dark.

🔍 PLANNING A WEDDING?

If the proposal gets a yes, brace yourself for a testing time. Wedding planning is a strain, and often falls hardest on the bride. A 2004 study by psychologist Debbie Ma in California, for instance, found that engaged women reported significantly higher levels of stress than non-engaged ones – though a good social support network could help to mitigate this somewhat. What's more, a study published in the *Journal of Feminist Family Therapy* in 2009 reported that while many couples turned to wedding planning books for guidance, the books tended to give advice that "promotes inequality" – meaning that women were doing most of the work, which is hardly relaxing!

🕐 A DAZZLING SLOGAN

"A Diamond Is Forever" is the phrase that *Advertising Age* called the best slogan of the 20th century: it was coined in 1947 by copywriter Frances Gerety, for the De Beers diamond company. We can also thank the jewellery industry for the convention that a diamond should cost a man two months' salary. In fact the tradition of diamond engagement rings only became popular in America in the late 19th century after the discovery of South African diamond mines, and the only people who insist they're essential are the diamond-sellers themselves. If you prefer a less expensive ring, or no ring at all, there's no reason to feel obligated.

✓ TOP TEN TRIVIA

While you're waiting for that proposal, some popular statistics – best taken with a pinch of salt:

1 **95 per cent of US brides have an engagement ring,** though the number is falling, for both financial and ethical reasons (such as avoiding "blood diamonds").

2 **85 per cent** of women who have an engagement ring are given it **at the proposal.**

3 **42 per cent** of engaged couples **choose a ring together:** in 85 per cent of cases, the man pays for it.

4 **57 per cent of men say buying the ring is stressful.**

5 **45 per cent of men do no research** before buying the ring.

6 **75 per cent** of engagement rings are **diamond solitaires.**

7 **$74 billion** is spent on diamonds each year by consumers in 34 countries around the globe.

8 **48 per cent** of women want a **surprise proposal.**

9 **13–14 months** is the average length of an engagement in the USA and the UK.

10 **New York's Yankee Stadium** boasts at least **one marriage proposal on the scoreboard every game.** However, they also report that they get someone "frantically" calling to cancel the scheduled proposal at least five times a year!

CHAPTER 5
TOGETHER
ON THE ROAD TO LASTING LOVE

ARE WE GOING TO LAST?
WHAT YOUR CONVERSATIONS PREDICT

Can you tell whether a relationship is going to be happy ever after or end badly? According to some researchers, you can – and with startling accuracy. It all comes down to how you talk to each other.

In 1986, American psychologist John Gottman was busy in his "Love Lab" with his colleague Robert Levenson, wiring newlyweds to electrodes and asking them to discuss stressful and joyful aspects of their relationships. Six years later, Gottman saw the couples again. Some were happily married; some were either together but miserable or had broken up entirely.

What was the difference between them? The couples who were still happily married had shown low heart rates and stress signals during the 1986 tests, while the unhappy ones had looked calm on the surface but showed pounding hearts, sweating, and tension.

Masters and disasters

Gottman dubbed the first group "masters" and the second "disasters", and then tried to identify what made the masters so masterly. In 1990, for instance, he placed couples in a "love lab" that was designed to feel more like a holiday retreat than a place of study and invited 130 newly married couples to spend the day there, doing ordinary domestic tasks, chatting, and acting as normal. In effect, he was observing couples "in the wild".

Throughout their time together, couples make "bids" – calls for each other's attention that angle for a positive response. They may be small on the surface ("Hey look, a bird!"), but they attempt to create a moment of connection. Partners can either "turn towards" or "turn away" from a bid. ("Oh yes, how pretty!" versus "Leave me be, I'm reading the paper.") No

HAPPY

SOON-TO-DIVORCE

KEEP IT POSITIVE

According to Gottman's research, the magic ratio is 5 to 1: couples who have five times as many positive interactions as negative are likely to be stable. In the unstable couples who later broke up, for every eight positive interactions, there were ten negatives ones – a ratio of 0.8 to 1. How do your ratios look?

HEY, GREAT NEWS!

A 2006 study at UCLA found that responding positively to situations where things go well can be as important as how you respond to negative events. Suppose a wife tells her husband she's got a big promotion: how does he respond? Of the four options below, only active-constructive makes people feel really happy in a relationship.

Response Type	Behaviour	Example
Active-constructive	Enthusiastic support	"That's wonderful! Your hard work's really paying off. What's the new job going to involve?"
Passive-constructive	Quiet, understated support	"That's nice, darling."
Active-destructive	Spoiling the event	"Are you sure you can handle that? You struggled a lot in your last job."
Passive-destructive	Ignoring the event	"That reminds me, your mother called. Could you call her back?"

one turns towards every single bid – everyone's preoccupied sometimes – but the disasters turned towards each other's bids 33 per cent of the time, in stark contrast to the masters' 87 per cent. The successful couples, in other words, were meeting each other's bids at a high rate. Gottman estimated he could predict a couple's chances of staying together on this basis with up to 94 per cent accuracy.

Accentuating the positive

The central difference in attitude between masters and disasters, Gottman thinks, is what people are on the watch for. Masters are looking for opportunities to be pleased with their partners, while disasters are on the lookout for mistakes.

It's the old enemy self-verification again (see pages 32–33): we tend to selectively notice things that fit in with our expectations, and pay less attention to things that contradict it.

If we expect a relationship to go badly, then we're highly vigilant for signs that it might – which means we notice everything our partner does wrong. If we can believe that we're essentially lovable and our partners are essentially good, we're far more likely to notice their good points, recognize their "bids" as a sign that they want to feel close to us, and create a positive cycle.

Masters are, to quote Gottman, "building this culture of respect and appreciation very purposefully". To be a master, treat harmony as something that you can build on a foundation of thanks, compliments, and affirmations. Meeting a partner's bids positively – and looking out for moments when they are especially nice, thoughtful, or impressive so you can call attention to them – creates a relationship that has a much better chance of lasting, and which feels calmer, warmer, and kinder for both of you.

80%

Gottman reports that a **breakdown of intimacy** is described as the leading cause of **80 per cent of divorces.**

7-year-itch?

The commonest times for a **marriage to end** are either at **5–7 years,** due to a high level of **conflict,** or at **15–16 years,** due to a **lack of emotional connection.**

STAYING CONNECTED

LITTLE EXERCISES IN HAPPINESS

When we're used to each other, it can be easy to take the connection for granted, but actually you'll enjoy the relationship a lot more if you put a bit of conscious effort into your time together.

Love should go without saying? Far from it: what we don't say, we can often forget to think and feel. It might feel a little strange, at first, to do exercises in romantic connection, but try approaching them as a gift or as a game to share with each other. You may be surprised, whether you've been a couple for a while or you've only recently got together.

🖉 A WEEK OF KINDNESS

There's nothing like appreciation to make a relationship feel worthwhile.

1 **Each get yourself a private notebook** or memo pad, which, for the moment, you don't show your partner.

2 **Every day for a week**, make a note of everything your partner does that makes you feel appreciated, respected, valued, or special – even the small things like saying, "I'm making a cup of tea, would you like one?" Big or small, the only criterion is that these things mean something to you.

3 **At the end of the week,** take a quiet moment somewhere, sit down together, and exchange your lists – not as debts, of course, but as gifts.

4 **Keep doing this for several weeks.** Make a note of any trends that emerge: you may very well find yourselves developing some positively rewarding patterns!

BEFORE I MET YOU

Sometimes it's good to be reminded how being together has improved your lives. Try making a list along these lines:

1 **Sit together to do this exercise.** You'll be writing things down and then reading them out, so both have access to a convenient surface.

2 **Head a piece of paper "Until I met you".** Add two subheadings: "No one saw me as…" and "I was afraid I wouldn't…".

3 **Fill in everything that your partner changed** about how you felt others saw you and what you were afraid wouldn't happen to meet your needs. You can go right back to childhood for this one.

Happy marriages are based on a deep friendship. By this I mean a mutual respect for and enjoyment of each other's company.

John Gottman
American psychotherapist and psychology professor

 ## NOTHING TO SAY?

Sometimes we feel too tired to communicate: there's nothing we can think of to say, even though we may want a bit of attention and closeness. If you want to touch base but you're stuck for a topic, try this exercise:

1 **Sit facing each other in a comfortable position.** Close your eyes, and do a mindful breathing or loving-kindness meditation, whichever you feel more in need of at that moment (see page 56).

2 **At an agreed signal** – you might like to set an alarm so neither of you has to worry about being the time-keeper – open your eyes. Study each other's face, without speaking.

3 **When you feel ready to begin talking**, meet your partner's gaze and smile. If your partner does this first and you want to keep looking for a while more, gently shake your head. This is not a rejection but a way of asking for more time. Give each other the gift of space and only begin when you're both ready.

4 **One of you (agree which before you start) speaks.** You're going to have a conversation with only one phrase; it should be a short, truthful, neutral, and peaceful sentence such as "It rained yesterday."

5 **When one of you says the phrase**, the other replies, "Yes."

6 **The starting partner repeats the phrase**, and the other continues to answer, "Yes." As you continue, you may find all sorts of emotions inflect your words this way and that: communicate with each other through tone of voice. You'll find you can hold a tender conversation even when you have "nothing to say".

 ## PHYSICAL CLOSENESS

Missing intimacy but not in the mood for sex? Try this shared breathing meditation:

1 **Lay some sturdy cushions** on the floor so you can sit comfortably on them for 15 minutes.

2 **You and your partner** sit down on the cushions, cross-legged or in whatever position works for you, leaning against each other back-to-back.

3 **Resting your weight lightly** against each other (you should be relaxed, but not so slumped that your partner feels squashed), do a mindful breathing meditation (see page 56). As you meditate, focus your attention on the sensation not just of your own breath, but of the rhythm of your partner's breathing as you feel their body expand and contract against yours.

THE SCIENCE OF MEDITATION

Meditation has long been practised in Eastern religion, but Western science is becoming increasingly convinced of its therapeutic value. In a study at Harvard Medical School, for instance, fMRI scans showed that meditation lit up parts of the brain that regulate blood pressure and manage stress. A study published in *Psychological Science* in 2013 found that eight weeks' meditation measurably increased subjects' compassionate responses. It seems that meditation really can make you a calmer, more caring person!

THE POWER OF VULNERABILITY

TAKING A RISK ON TRUE UNDERSTANDING

In the quest for love that lasts, we may worry whether we're really worthy of love. Actually, letting go of that idea and considering ourselves inherently worthy may be one of the most lovable things you ever do.

Once we get into a relationship it can be difficult to shed the assumption that being loved depends on being worthy of love, and that if we let our imperfections show, we won't be loved after all. No one is perfect: how do some people manage to be loved despite their faults?

Feeling worthy

According to American therapist and researcher Brené Brown, the central skill is an ability to be vulnerable. Her term for this ability is being "whole-hearted": people who can overcome their fear of shame – of being found lacking and getting rejected – are people who accept their own identity without expecting perfection. Whole-hearted people are courageous in owning themselves, faults and all, compassionate towards themselves as well as others, and willing to accept they can only relate to other people as their real self rather than the self they feel they should be.

For Brown, the biggest hindrance to connection is that shame and anxiety are painful, so we prefer to numb them out – but it's impossible to numb feelings selectively. If we switch off when we feel vulnerable, chances are that when there's reason to feel joyful or grateful, we struggle to switch back on again. Embracing ourselves as flawed people and accepting that there will be scary moments in life is the best way to keep ourselves open to real and rewarding love.

Who to trust?

The risk of opening up is that we may expose ourselves to someone who isn't very supportive: if we aren't treated sympathetically, we're likely to end up feeling worse. We need a partner who welcomes our admission of vulnerability as a sign of trust and is prepared to respond with openness and vulnerability of their own. It's common sense that empathy helps make relationships satisfying, and the research backs this up.

A UK study in 2010, for example, found that of 149 couples, those who felt their partners to be empathic were not only happier in their relationships, but also less prone to depression. When you admit to a partner that you're feeling vulnerable, how they take the news is a big predictor of happiness or otherwise.

The best approach is to treat each other's vulnerability as an occasion of mutual respect. Showing our fragility takes courage: the person who never shows weakness is, psychologically speaking, probably more frightened than the person who can admit it. A partner who can admit they're flawed and want love anyway is exactly the person to share life's challenges with, so support each other for your courage and trust that it will make you stronger, not weaker, to admit that you're not always perfect.

EMPATHY

We're often urged to empathize, but what exactly does that mean? You can understand how another person is feeling without caring, while sympathy – feeling sorry for someone – doesn't necessarily bring understanding. With empathy, we understand, we share someone's feelings, and we care. Having all three skills – shown here in Dr Shari Young Kuchenbecker's model – allows us to connect well with others and feel as they feel, so that "I" versus "you" becomes "we".

1 Discrimination and labelling Correctly identifying someone's feelings.

2 Assuming perspective Being able to imagine yourself in someone else's situational shoes.

3 Emotional capacity Sharing someone's feelings and responsively caring about their emotions, sensations, experiences.

✕ WHEN A PARTNER FEELS VULNERABLE

What NOT to do when a partner admits they're feeling vulnerable:

✱ **Compete.** You're bound to have vulnerabilities of your own, of course, but your partner talking about theirs doesn't diminish yours. Getting into one-downmanship defeats the point. Only share yours to show support, or wait your turn; there will be other moments to ask for support of your own.

✱ **Score points.** If your partner admits they acted unreasonably because they were feeling vulnerable, don't jump in and say, "See, I told you you were being unreasonable!" That's a pretty dependable way to discourage them confiding in you a second time.

✱ **Go in hyper-rational.** The thing they're worried about may be, logically, not a very big deal, but don't try to debate them into feeling that way – you'll probably make them feel invalidated. It's much more reassuring to just listen and assure them you care.

✱ **Try to "fix" them.** You can't fix being human. A desire to help is good, but trying to persuade your partner to change their attitude or their personality just makes them feel rejected.

✱ **Break confidences.** Sometimes it's helpful to discuss relationship problems with friends, but don't talk over anything private without your partner's permission.

🔍 DO YOU UNDERSTAND ME?

When we need empathy, what helps us most? According to a 2012 study published in the *Journal of Family Psychology*, it varies by gender (at least in heterosexual couples). For both sexes, romantic satisfaction was helped by having a partner who could read their negative emotions accurately, but men in particular were most happy when they were able to read their wife's positive emotions accurately. We all want understanding and sympathy; despite the stereotypes, perhaps men particularly want approval from their loved ones.

IN ORDER FOR CONNECTION TO HAPPEN, WE HAVE TO ALLOW OURSELVES TO BE SEEN, REALLY SEEN

BRENÉ BROWN, RESEARCH PROFESSOR OF SOCIAL WORK, UNIVERSITY OF HOUSTON

YOU BRING OUT THE BEST IN ME
THE MICHELANGELO EFFECT

Is love a science or an art? Science suggests that being a loving partner is close to being its own kind of art form – like a creative genius, we can "sculpt" our partner into their best self, and vice versa.

There's a possibly apocryphal story about the Renaissance artist Michelangelo: asked how he had created an extraordinary statue, he replied, "I saw an angel in the marble and carved until I set him free." We'd all love a partner who could do the same for us: see deep into our souls, find our best selves, and help set them free. Recent research suggests that it's more realistic than we might think.

Sculpting each other
What psychologists have dubbed the "Michelangelo effect" is a specific type of behaviour confirmation. Put simply, we tend to act in ways that accord with how we see ourselves (see self-verification on pages 32–33), and our partners' expectations of us have an influence on our self-image. A loving partner – a Michelangelo – will respond to you in ways that move you closer to your ideal self.

How does behaviour confirmation work? Carrying certain expectations of us, partners tend to shape situations to support those expectations by creating or heading off certain opportunities for us. If, for instance, your partner sees you as an artistic person, they're more likely to buy you drawing paper for your birthday, take the kids out for the day so you can paint, and show off your work to family and friends. Given these opportunities to explore your artistic side, it's likely that your skill will improve, your understanding of art will deepen, and you too will see yourself as artistic, as that's how you're being treated.

The same partner, though, may see you as dreamy and impractical, and so always do the map-reading when you're lost, sort out your tax return, and be a little sceptical if you offer to fix that broken tap. Psychology calls this "selective instigation". If these assumptions head off opportunities for you to act in practical ways, you may grow more reliant on your partner, feel less confident about your handyman abilities, and get out of practice with certain skills.

More subtly, we also tend to pick up emotional cues from our partner: if we are effusive, for example, and they are less so, if we express anger vigorously and they hate yelling, if we're the worrying sort and they are more laid back, the responses we give to each other will push both partners in new directions, through "selective reinforcement" (see opposite). How a partner feels about us is something that most of us are aware of fairly constantly, and we adapt to keep those feelings positive. We are, in other words, "sculpting" each other.

> When our partners can chisel and polish us in a way that helps us to achieve our ideal self, that's a wonderful thing.
>
> **Eli Finkel**
> Social psychology professor,
> Northwestern University

SELECTIVE REINFORCEMENT

The concept of shaping our partners by using rewards – or punishments – may sound as if we're Pavlovian dogs, rather than consenting adults, but we can bring our awareness to the process...

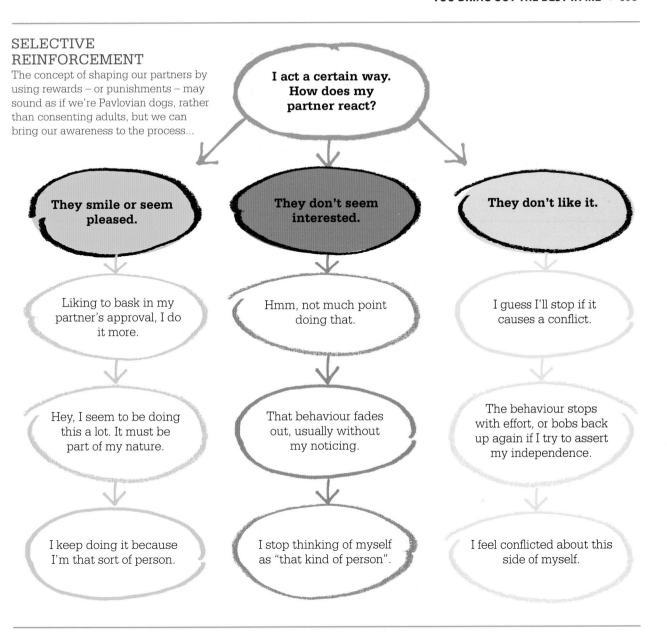

I act a certain way. How does my partner react?

They smile or seem pleased.

They don't seem interested.

They don't like it.

Liking to bask in my partner's approval, I do it more.

Hmm, not much point doing that.

I guess I'll stop if it causes a conflict.

Hey, I seem to be doing this a lot. It must be part of my nature.

That behaviour fades out, usually without my noticing.

The behaviour stops with effort, or bobs back up again if I try to assert my independence.

I keep doing it because I'm that sort of person.

I stop thinking of myself as "that kind of person".

I feel conflicted about this side of myself.

Realizing the ideal

The prospect of being "sculpted" by a partner may sound a little unnerving: who wants to be treated as mere raw material? With the right partner, though, we experience the deeply rewarding Michelangelo effect. Most of us have an ideal image of who we want to be and feel a fair amount of regret that we don't seem to be that person. If we have a loving partner who sees in us the "self" that we really want to be, just being around them supports us in becoming that person. Of all the qualities we should look for in a partner, perhaps one of the most important is that they should see us as the person we hope to be – because just by seeing us that way, they help make it happen.

TWO HALVES, OR TWO WHOLES?

HOW TO AVOID GETTING STUCK IN STEREOTYPES

There's a comfort in familiarity, and every couple develops their routines and roles. Making too many assumptions, though, can undermine real connection, so it's worth checking you're still sure who's who.

When you first meet your beloved, it can feel like you're embarking on an endless voyage of discovery. After a few years together, though, you've probably grown fairly familiar with each other. You've heard each other's life stories, and their favourite jokes, and you begin to feel "settled". If the relationship is warm and affectionate this can, of course, be very comforting – but sometimes we can be a little too complacent in our assumptions.

I'm the red one, you're the green one

Do any of the following scenarios sound familiar to you?

- **You and your partner are on a drive** or a hike somewhere and lose your way. You pull out the map, and one of you automatically starts reading it with no question on either side as to who's the "map reader" of the relationship.
- **A new neighbour moves in** and you have a parcel that was left for them. This is a chance to introduce yourselves as a couple: one of you is definitely the front man – or woman – when it comes to this kind of thing, so that's the one who goes over with the parcel and says hello.
- **Your car breaks down** with its rooftop open to the rain. Both of you are struggling to fix the problem when a kind stranger pulls up and offers to help. One of you automatically stops working and starts talking to the stranger while the other continues to work on the roof: there's a "technical one" and a "sociable one" in this relationship and you both know which is which.

If you feel a wry amusement at any of these scenarios, you and your partner have definitely acquired certain roles. Now, it may be that actually neither of you is especially good at map reading or car repairs: to be the navigator, mechanic, or socialite of a relationship, the only requirement is that you be slightly better at it than your partner. (Or slightly more willing to do it.) The rest follows automatically and unplanned. You give the job to the person who's better at it or who prefers it, and over time, this simply becomes a law of nature: one of you is good at X, the other at Y.

A bit too familiar

There's nothing wrong with allocating everyday tasks according to preference, but there can be two disadvantages if you get typecast. The first is the effect on you as an individual: you may actually find yourself losing skills for lack of practice, and if you have insecurities about your abilities, your relationship roles can unintentionally reinforce them (see pages 192–193).

The second is that you limit the opportunities to surprise each other – and once you do that, you limit the romance. Try some of the exercises on this page and see if you can still be "new-found" to each other – as you were when you first embarked on that endless voyage of discovery.

> Two halves don't make a whole. Two wholes make a whole.
>
> **Jason Mraz,**
> American singer-songwriter

 **THE OLD NEW**

When you were first together, did you discover new things because your partner was interested in them? There's no reason to stop doing that. Try one or more of the following:

- **Is there anything you used to do** or anywhere you used to go before you met, which you haven't done much since? Try it again, and this time bring your partner along.

- **Is there something that you've always wanted to do** but never got round to? Sit down with your partner and each make your own list, then merge them together.

- **You don't have to do everything on the list,** but pick out a few that you'd be really interested in and make some definite plans to do them.

 OH, I'D NEVER DO THAT!

Is there something you'd like to do but don't because your partner wouldn't want to? Remind yourself you're an individual, not just half of a couple.

1 **Each make a list of these ideas.** You may find your ideas interest each other more than you expected, but if they really don't mesh, it's time to schedule some "me-time".

2 **Pick a day when you'll each go off and do your own thing.** (Or, if you have kids to look after, pick a weekend and take one day each.)

3 **At the end of the day,** when it's time to share what it was like, meet somewhere nice, such as a restaurant, as if for a date with someone new. You will each, after all, be meeting someone who's had a new experience!

 WHO IS THE "COPER"?

Is one of you the emotional one and the other the peacemaker? Long term, you'll both need reasonable coping skills. German psychologist Britta Busch looked at how older couples faced changes to their routines in retirement, and found three types of copers: positive, negative, and indifferent (one partner coping positively, the other not). Key traits were:

POSITIVE
- ✔ **Signalling stress clearly**
- ✔ **Relationship satisfaction**
- ✔ **Life satisfaction**
- ✔ **Harmony with their partner**

NEGATIVE
- ✘ **Communicating indirectly**
- ✘ **Communicating aggressively**
- ✘ **High levels of anxiety**
- ✘ **Frequent anger**

Busch found that it was, of course, the positive couples who felt more confident about coping in retirement. If your partner seems to be better at managing stress than you, you might want to brush up your skills before you have to spend all your days together!

THE WORST IDEAS OF ALL
WHAT YOU REALLY MUST AVOID

Every couple runs into conflict sometimes. Usually we can just disagree, but some ways of disagreeing are destructive while others can lead to reconciliation. What are the best ways to get the second outcome?

We want our partners to love and approve of us at all times, but sometimes they have angry things to say and we have to hear them out or they'll never be satisfied. That's a pretty unpleasant experience even for the happiest couple – but what's the difference between a couple that can fight and make up and a couple that can't stop spiralling downwards?

The Four Horsemen
John Gottman identifies four destructive behaviours that he refers to as the "Four Horsemen of the Apocalypse": according to Gottman, just their presence alone can predict divorce with up to 80 per cent accuracy. These horsemen are:

1 Criticism
We may have trenchant comments about our partner's behaviour, but there's clearly a difference between criticizing what someone does and what someone is. "You keep leaving the dishes to me and it's annoying me" is a complaint but fair comment. "You keep leaving the dishes to me – you're so lazy and selfish!" is personal criticism. Psychologists find that the second approach is commoner with women than with men – either way, it doesn't help.

2 Contempt
Criticism can escalate to a complete dismissal of the other person. There are many ways of expressing disrespect for your partner, from rolling your eyes, making mean "jokes", or sneering, to aggressive verbal assaults. However it's expressed, contempt is profoundly wounding and spells serious trouble for a relationship: how can you come to a resolution with someone who is making it clear they think you're worthless?

3 Defensiveness
No one likes having their faults pointed out, but the more defensive

START SOFTLY, STAY POSITIVE

Does a "soft start-up" guarantee a good response? Sadly no: even if you raise your point gently, your partner may still get defensive or upset. If you run into that problem, Dr Julie Schwartz Gottman of the Gottman Institute recommends holding on to your patience and saying, as gently as you can, something like "Honey, I'm not trying to criticize you here. I really do care about you, I just want to be closer to you." So many arguments do include criticism that your partner might be expecting it when you raise a grievance; a bit of reassurance can help to ease their tension so you can then talk about things positively.

you are, the more you slam the shutters – and when you do that, you'll have difficulty taking in what your partner is actually saying, because you're too busy shoring up your own case. Excuses, denying responsibility, and making counter-accusations are all examples of defensiveness.

? WHAT'S YOUR CONFLICT STYLE?

1 Gottman identifies three different kinds of people when it comes to arguments. See if you recognize you or your partner's tendencies in any of these:

(There's some overlap with attachment styles here – soothers are often secure, attackers often anxious, and avoiders often avoidant – but it's not an exact match, so go by the individual.)

Soothers:
people who want to smooth things over with as much reassurance as possible.

Avoiders:
people who'd rather deflect an issue than thrash it out.

Attackers:
people who go in on the offensive.

2 **Which is the best style?** Actually, couples often do well when each partner has the same style. It's the mismatches below that can create misunderstandings:

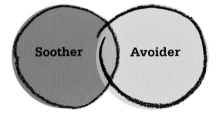

Soother/Avoider:
Avoiders can find soothers overwhelming and retreat, leaving the couple stuck in an endless round of pursuer and pursued.

Soother **Attacker**

Soother/Attacker:
Both styles are highly emotional – if they can't influence each other, they both end up frustrated.

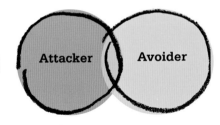

Attacker/Avoider:
The worst combination of all: like soother/avoider, there's a pursuer-and-pursued dynamic, but with this pairing it's highly aggressive and painful to both.

4 **Stonewalling**
This method – more popular with men – consists of refusing to respond. Your partner gets more and more upset, and you stare into space as if they're not even there. In effect, you are saying, "I'm not in this relationship as long as things aren't going my way." Once you adopt this attitude, you may find, emotionally speaking, it's hard to get back in again.

Can we avoid the horsemen?
To avoid a conflict escalating beyond repair, the Gottman Institute advises using a "soft start-up". Rather than going in guns blazing (which will only goad your partner into taking cover or firing back), keep your complaint within moderate bounds:

- Complain, but don't get personal.
- Use "I" statements: "I'm upset" rather than "You're upsetting me."

- Be descriptive rather than judgmental: "I had to do all the chores today" rather than "You always leave the chores to me."
- Be polite and show appreciation when you can.

If you can begin your objection softly and stay positive as far as possible (see opposite), you stand a much better chance of resolving things to your mutual satisfaction.

ARGUING LIKE GROWN-UPS
HOW TO COMMUNICATE, NOT MANIPULATE

Have you ever had one of those arguments where it feels like you can't do anything right? Do you ever feel like you're both stuck in a script rather than talking sensibly? Maybe it's time to check your roles.

In 1964, a book of post-Freudian theory by psychiatrist Dr Eric Berne was published. *Games People Play* advanced a "transactional analysis" of human relationships. The idea is that there are three mental stages we can occupy: the "parent" state, concerned with external rules ("Don't touch the oven", "Say please"); the "child" state, which comes with our dawning self-awareness and is concerned with our feelings; and the "adult" state, which makes decisions based on observing the world. We are not always the same psychological age in all our dealings: sometimes we shift from age to age and role to role.

In a conflict with our partner, we hope we can talk like two adults, but it's easy to slip into a parental role ("You know you should have told me about the office party sooner...") and/or a child one ("...I can't read your mind – it's not fair!"). That makes it hard to resolve things as equals. If one partner slips into a child or parent role, it's easy for the other to slip into the complementary one: if someone whines at us like a child, we want to snap at them like a parent, and vice versa. With both sides feeling wronged, an argument soon turns into a fight. Getting a grip on our own maturity and exercising self-control in the hopes of encouraging our partner to do likewise can take an effort!

The drama triangle
An added complication is the idea of victimization. Berne's pupil Stephen Karpman created a diagram known as the "Karpman drama triangle" (see left), to show three basic positions:

The Victim, a helpless innocent who's not responsible for anything that happens to them.

The Persecutor, an aggressor who coerces the Victim.

🔍 GOING ROUND IN CIRCLES?

You may be stuck in a Karpman drama triangle, driving each other round these three roles:

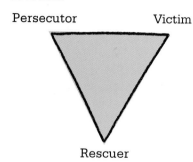

Persecutor   Victim

Rescuer

In reality, the Victim isn't wholly innocent, the Persecutor isn't completely powerful, and the Rescuer isn't entirely helpful: each role just validates the false position of the others. Sometimes, of course, people really are innocent victims, malign bullies, and heroic rescuers – but if your relationship isn't outright abusive (see pages 156–157), it's more likely that you're two fallible human beings who've fallen into playing those roles rather than communicating constructively.

SWITCHING ROLES

When we argue, we can shuttle around Karpman's drama triangle, pushing our opponent off one point and onto another. If you get stuck in this pattern, you might want to take a minute and get some space – as long as it's mutually agreed, not storming out – and then try some affirmation instead.

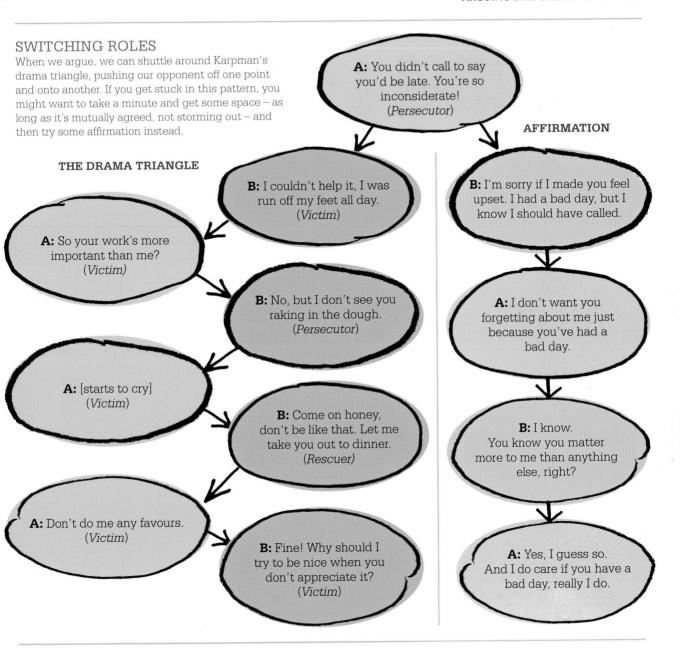

THE DRAMA TRIANGLE

AFFIRMATION

A: You didn't call to say you'd be late. You're so inconsiderate! (*Persecutor*)

B: I couldn't help it, I was run off my feet all day. (*Victim*)

A: So your work's more important than me? (*Victim*)

B: No, but I don't see you raking in the dough. (*Persecutor*)

A: [starts to cry] (*Victim*)

B: Come on honey, don't be like that. Let me take you out to dinner. (*Rescuer*)

A: Don't do me any favours. (*Victim*)

B: Fine! Why should I try to be nice when you don't appreciate it? (*Victim*)

B: I'm sorry if I made you feel upset. I had a bad day, but I know I should have called.

A: I don't want you forgetting about me just because you've had a bad day.

B: I know. You know you matter more to me than anything else, right?

A: Yes, I guess so. And I do care if you have a bad day, really I do.

The Rescuer, a saviour who intervenes to help or save the Victim.

In this kind of argument, someone will usually switch from position to position, depending on the reactions of another person, and if we get caught up in it, we tend to fall into complementary roles – see above. It can be obscurely rewarding to play these roles: in Berne's terminology, we seek people to provide "strokes" – gestures of acknowledgment that we're there. Validating someone's role by playing up to it is a stroke of sorts. It's better long term, though, to move away from these roles into direct communication, adult to adult. If someone's feeling insecure enough to get into this drama triangle (people who've had difficult childhoods are particularly prone to it), they do need "strokes" – but what they really need is honest affirmations of love. If you get into conflict, keep an eye on how you respond, and if you find you're falling into the same old pattern, try affirming each other more directly.

A GOOD CLEAN FIGHT
HOW TO ARGUE AND MOVE ON

We'd all like to avoid conflict if we could, but let's admit it: sometimes we're annoying and sometimes we get annoyed. How do we thrash things out with a partner without ending up unhappier than ever?

We may try to settle important issues by peaceful negotiation and constructive discussion, but everyone has a bad day sometimes. Being able to express anger with each other is probably healthy – you're not afraid of your partner, for one thing – but in the end it's important to settle the issue rather than stay angry. What's the best way to manage that – try to engage your partner actively, or to disengage and let things cool off?

Step up or step back?
The answer depends very much on how threatened your partner feels. According to US studies published in 2013 in the *Journal of Social and Clinical Psychology*, fights can be viewed as having two different bases: perceived neglect, and perceived threat. If your partner is angry, it's useful to ask yourself whether their anger boils down to "Don't you talk to me like that!" (perceived threat) or "Stop ignoring me!" (perceived neglect): these grievances have opposite solutions (see below) and the wrong one may only escalate things.

Collaborate or compete?
Some couples are more cooperative than others, and you'd think that a collaborative style – actively working together to build trust and emotional closeness – would make for a happier relationship. But even if a couple tries to deal with conflict collaboratively, it's still stressful.

So where does that leave us? In 2006, psychologist Jeremy Tiegerman met with couples in a conflict resolution programme: he theorized that the collaborative couples would be happier with each other than the competitive ones. In fact, the results

Perceived threat:
"Don't you talk to me like that!"

How to resolve:
Disengage from your anger.

Lower the tone: soften your voice, keep your body language unthreatening.

WHY ARE YOU SO ANGRY?
If someone is yelling at you, it doesn't mean they don't feel threatened: threat triggers the "fight or flight" response, and sometimes we meet a threat by facing it down.

Perceived neglect:
"Stop ignoring me!"

How to resolve:
Engage with your partner.

LAUGH IT OFF

Does it help to make jokes in an argument? It depends what kind. A US study published in 2013 in the *Personality and Social Psychology Bulletin* videotaped couples trying to solve a relationship conflict, assessed their attachment styles, and classified three kinds of humour:

Type of humour (and who uses it)	Characterized by jokes that...	Representing a bid for...
Affiliative humour (most typical of secure types)	invite the partner to share the amusement	connection
Self-defeating humour (most typical of anxious types)	put the teller down	reassurance
Aggressive humour (most typical of avoidant types)	are funny at the partner's expense	dominance

Neither aggressive nor self-defeating humour tended to get a good response, especially when the teller's partner was very distressed – affiliative humour proved the most effective.

were unexpected: the style of conflict management didn't make very much difference. What mattered was how often, and how intensely, the couples came into conflict. More fights made for less happiness no matter how the couples dealt with it. Perhaps naturally competitive people are just as comfortable with competition as collaborative ones are with collaboration: the key finding, though, is that it's probably best to try to solve problems before they get to the point of turning into a quarrel.

Virtually everyone has fights, but it's good to remember that different fights may be about different needs – and that it's usually a good idea to keep the number of quarrels to a minimum if you can!

Avoid being adversarial: stop trying to gain your point, at least for now.

Relinquish power: let your partner have their say, and concede whatever you can.

Be open to your partner expressing their feelings, accent the positive ones, and communicate yours.

Show more open affection and demonstrate your investment in both the relationship and the conversation.

OUTLASTING THE QUARRELS

What can long-married couples teach us? In a study published in the journal *Psychotherapy: Theory, Research, Practice, Training* in 2000, researchers led by Richard A. Mackey at Boston College interviewed 72 couples from diverse backgrounds who'd been together for about 35 years, in order to see how they handled conflict resolution. The conclusion was that long-lasting couples tended to be able to explore each other's needs and expectations and accept each other's differences: a bit of empathy in advance can save a lot of conflict. No couple will agree on everything, and if you agree on that, you've got a good start.

STOP HOGGING THE DUVET!

SHARING A BED

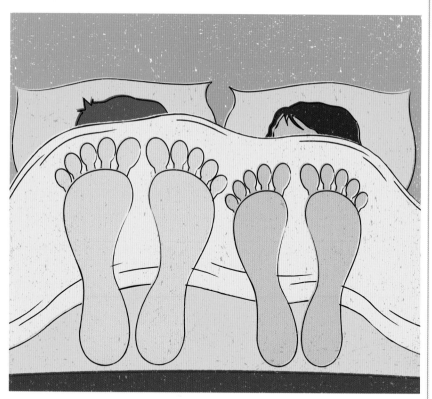

At the end of a long day, is the thought of curling up under the covers with your partner a welcome one? Some beds are a haven, some are a minefield. How do you keep everyone happy and get a good night's sleep?

The average adult needs between seven and nine hours sleep per night. If you share a bed with your partner, that's a substantial part of your lives that you'll spend in each other's exclusive, if unconscious, company. Few things are more intimate. Sleep is so vital to our wellbeing – even a single hour's "sleep debt" slows down our thinking and lowers our immune system – that sharing a bed can also affect how you relate by day. Conflict is best handled with constructive maturity, but no one is at their most grown-up if they've been woken up for the fifth time that night!

Closeness under the covers

Sleeping together can help physical intimacy, of course – it's easier to snuggle or seduce someone within reach – but we've long sought safety and warmth as well. Night-time is a nervous business for dim-sighted mammals like humans. Shared sleep offers a state of mutual protection that unites us against the night.

For this very reason, of course, some people aren't keen on it: people with avoidant attachment style, for instance, are particularly inclined to prefer a solitary bed. Not everyone who hesitates to bunk up is avoiding intimacy, though: sometimes they just need their rest.

I just need to sleep!

Maybe you have no difficulty in curling up and dozing off together, but one in three people suffers from insomnia at least now and again, and sometimes it is just easier to sleep if you don't have to worry about waking someone else up.

What if you're a morning person and your partner's a night owl, or vice versa? A US study of 150 couples, published in the *Journal of Marital and Family Therapy* in 1991, found that mismatched sleeping patterns

⚲ GOOD DAY, GOOD SLEEP

We can expect to get along better during the day if we've had a decent night's sleep – but there's also reason to believe that it works the other way around, too.

1 A good start. In a study at the University of Pittsburgh's Sleep Medicine Institute, researchers followed the sleep patterns of 29 co-sleeping couples for seven days, asking each partner to keep a sleep diary that week. The diaries made interesting reading: not only did the couples report getting on better if they'd slept well the previous night (especially the men), but both men and women (especially the women) also slept better after a harmonious day.

✔ **Our bedime routine** also affects how well we sleep. See the American Psychological Association website for some simple steps to better sleep: http://www.apa.org/helpcenter/sleep-disorders.aspx

2 Open up. A US study published in *Health Psychology* in 2014 reported that both men and women slept better if they'd experienced positive "self-disclosure" (or opening up) during the day: women said they felt their sleep quality was better, while men said they woke up fewer times during the night. Finding a good relationship pattern and a good sleep pattern can become a virtuous circle.

✔ **For more on self-disclosure,** see pages 175 and 188–189.

3 Don't go to bed angry. Even if you're tired, try to make up. In a US study published in the journal *Personal Relationships* in 2011, psychologists Angela Hicks and Lisa Diamond looked at 39 subjects who were in established relationships and found that all of them slept worse and woke unhappier the morning after an unresolved quarrel. The people most badly affected, though, were the highly anxious types. The least affected were the avoidants, suggesting that they were able to tamp down their emotions the most firmly – but even they had a bad night and felt low the next morning.

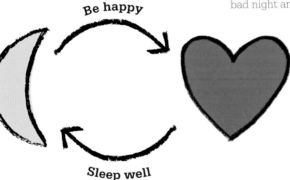

Be happy

Sleep well

✔ **For more on resolving a quarrel,** see pages 198–201.

do indeed cause problems: the couples who couldn't or wouldn't sleep at the same time were likely to have more arguments, less shared activity, and less sex. The ones who managed to avoid this downward spiral did so by being flexible and finding a compromise.

In the end, a good night's sleep is probably more important than whether you sleep together or apart. A 2013 study at the University of Pittsburgh found that people suffering from insomnia had a lot more difficulty processing negative emotions, while a 2010 UK study found that lack of sleep made people less inhibited and more impulsive in responding to negative stimuli. Tired people are irritable, in short, and have more difficulty avoiding a quarrel. Since we're also more likely to be honest and constructive with our partners when we're rested (see above), all in all it pays to get enough sleep, even if you have to be a bit flexible about where you sleep. There are other ways to create physical and emotional intimacy, but an under-slept partner might be a grump no matter what you try!

🌙 7-9 hours

The average adult needs **seven to nine hours' sleep** per night. If you share a bed with your partner, that's **a third of your life together!**

CAREER PRESSURES

MAINTAINING EQUALITY IN A CONFUSING WORLD

In a perfect world we could lie in our partner's arms all day and never have to worry about money – but we do, unfortunately, and the money isn't always equal. Time to settle a few old arguments…

An increasingly common buzzword today is "dual-career couples": that is, couples who both work to support the household, and who both aim for a career that provides interest as well as a paycheque. For many of us, the days when life could be divided between the "breadwinner" and the "homemaker" are long gone – not only because of equal rights but often because a couple or family can't manage on one income. With those roles up for grabs now, how balanced is the world really?

Keeping it fair

No matter how hard a day you've had, someone's got to do the laundry or you'll both look a mess tomorrow. According to a survey from the University of Wisconsin, 50 per cent of American men claim they do most or half of the housework, but 70 per cent of women claim they do it all – since the women were logging about 28 hours of housework per week while the men were logging 16, the case for the ladies looks stronger.

Depending on the hours you work, the length of your commute, and the state of your health, splitting the chores 50-50 may not be possible, but unacknowledged work is liable to cause resentment even if the split is relatively even. It's probably best, if your partner does do more of the housework than you, to acknowledge that fact and thank them rather than insist that you do as much.

All equal?

Heterosexual working couples do have to deal with an unequal world. According to a 2013 report by the Pew Research Center, American women earn 84 cents to the dollar

28:16 hours

Who does the housework?
In a 2013 Pew report in the USA, women did **28 hours per week** while men were logging **16 hours.**

How times change: in the USA in **1970,** the **combined average number of hours** worked by a couple was **52.4 hours a week** – 40 years on, in **2009,** it was found to be **63 hours** a week.

40 years

In **1970, 66 per cent** of couples had a **spouse at home.** Forty years later, in **2010,** the figure was closer to **40 per cent.**

84¢:$1

In the 2013, **women in the USA** were only earning **84 cents to the dollar** compared to **men.** In 1967, it was just 58 cents to the dollar.

---

compared to men. In a 1996 study of the pay gap's impact on 62 couples, psychologist Jennifer Lowell found that people who earned less than their partner, both men and women, tended to feel that their partner leveraged their income to get their way in shared decisions.

Equality of income is a massively touchy subject both politically and domestically, so do your best to keep it out of disagreements as much as possible: the link between a person's earnings and how they perceive their judgement and status within a relationship is a can of worms that may be best left unopened.

A united front
Inequality isn't easy for men, either, and tends to hit their self-esteem. A study published in the *Journal of Personality and Social Psychology* found that although women's self-esteem could generally survive having a more successful male partner, men tended to feel bad about themselves if the positions

were reversed. The expectation that men have to be more successful to be manly really isn't fair to anyone: it's hard for men to be shamed because they happen to have a successful partner, and it's hard for women to have their work devalued. It can be difficult for both men and women to feel inadequate if their partner is a big success, but remember that you aren't opponents: the common enemy is stereotypes that put pressure on you.

Busy couples may struggle to find time together, which is bad enough, but when you add in the potential for financial inequality – which afflicts both men and women in different ways – it's wise to try as hard as possible to keep money out of arguments and remember that you're a team. It can be hard to make the household work even on two incomes, but trust that you're each doing your best and support each other, and it will go better for both of you.

🔍 UNEQUAL PAY

A common argument about unequal pay is that women earn less because they work lower-paid jobs. In a study published in 2014, Harvard labour economist Claudia Goldin looked at wage gaps, and after adjusting for educational level, age, and the number of hours worked, she found that even the whitest-collar jobs were out of step. Female financial specialists only make 66 per cent of their male counterparts' salaries, female doctors 71 per cent, and female lawyers and judges 82 per cent.

For heterosexual men wondering whether their girlfriends or wives are getting things out of proportion if they say they feel short-changed – well, they probably aren't, so the more supportive you are, the better.

THE CHILD-FREE LIFE
CHOOSING NOT TO HAVE CHILDREN

If you and your partner don't want to have children, you can still enjoy a full, happy life together – despite what others may tell you. Still, there are some issues you'll need to consider.

CHILDREN MAKE A MARRIAGE WORK?

A study by American psychologists Susan Hoffman and Ronald Levant compared 32 couples aged 25–35 who planned to remain child-free and 20 couples of similar age who planned to have children within the next five years. The result: the two groups were equally happy and well-adjusted. The only distinction was that the women who did not plan to have children considered themselves less stereotyped than those who did. That was in 1985. With non-parenthood becoming an increasingly visible option, it's possible that women nowadays may feel it's less unconventional to remain child-free. Either way the results are good news: whether you plan to have children or not makes very little difference to how happy you are.

There's a phrase becoming increasingly familiar in popular culture: "child-free". A few generations ago, marriage almost inevitably meant children, but since the advent of reliable contraception, choosing to have a long-term romantic relationship that doesn't involve becoming parents has become a viable option – and a rising number of couples are taking it.

(For the involuntarily childless, it's clearly a different story: if you want to have children, but you're worried you can't, turn to pages 208–209.)

The biological clock
In a 2012 study of voluntarily child-free women by Gail DeLyser of the Institute for Clinical Social Work, Chicago, none of the women found that perimenopause (the period of declining fertility that precedes menopause proper) or menopause brought any regrets: they were just as happy with their decision once it was irrevocable as they had always been.

If you're in a child-free relationship and you have second thoughts – or you worry you might do later – you needn't assume the decision is set in stone: as clinical psychologist and author Christine Meinecke points out regarding child-free couples, "Couples can redefine a relationship as many times as they need to." If you and your partner disagree, good communication is obviously vital, as the stakes are high for both of you.

Are we being selfish?
The voluntarily child-free often point out that there's nothing particularly selfish about choosing not to have children if you don't want them: after all, people generally have children

> ...the child-free, as a group, are not homogenous in their motivations
>
> **Vincent Ciaccio**
> Researcher in social psychology, Rutgers University

A GROWING MINORITY

Having children is still the "norm", though less so now than it was for our parents. In 2012, a National Health Statistics Report on fertility found that 57.4 per cent of US women aged 15–44 had children, and 42.6 per cent did not. Of those who were childless, 34.3 per cent were temporarily childless but open to having children later, 2.3 per cent were unable to have children, and 6 per cent were child-free by choice.

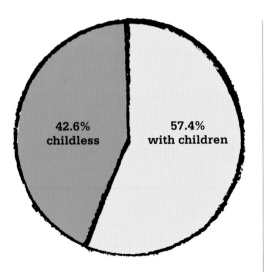

42.6% childless

57.4% with children

1 in 5

According to a Pew report in 2010, **one in five women** in the USA will have **no children in her lifetime,** compared to **one in 10 women in the 1970s.** UK figures from the Office for National Statistics are almost identical: one in five, and one in nine respectively.

34.3%

TEMPORARY

6%

VOLUNTARY

2.3%

INVOLUNTARY

24%

The **most educated women** are among the most likely never to have a child: in 2008, **24 per cent** (almost one in four) of American women aged 40–44 **with a higher degree** had not had children.

---

because of their own wishes, which isn't any more unselfish as a motivation. A study by Vincent Ciaccio, published in 2003, found that among the 457 volunteers who were interviewed, the reasons for choosing to avoid parenthood varied widely – careers, financial freedom, privacy, social lives, and the quality of their relationship with their partner were all common explanations.

As Ciaccio put it, "These reasons show a solid understanding of the responsibilities of parenthood, which the child-free do not desire to take

upon themselves." Child-free couples, in other words, are usually sensible people who have taken stock of their choices and arrived at a considered decision – it's not the only legitimate decision to take, of course, but it's as legitimate as any other.

A little support

Being voluntarily child-free is, according to the evidence, not a particularly regrettable decision. It's worth acknowledging, though, that it's still a minority choice, and child-free couples may well come under pressure from outsiders to change

their minds. If you're feeling that pressure yourself, you'll find many child-free support groups online. To the more mild-mannered child-free couple, the tone may often sound rather heated (the Net not being the home of the temperate). Even so, if your inclinations are against parenthood, but sympathetic to parents, and if you can find the kind of support that suits you, it will probably make your life easier.

In short, there's no reason to think that remaining a couple rather than a couple-plus-children is any worse a choice: your relationship is unlikely to suffer as long as you both remain comfortable with your decision.

TRYING FOR A BABY

KEEPING IT FUN WHEN THINGS GET SERIOUS

There can be a world of difference between love-making and trying for a baby – one of those sounds a lot more fun than the other. How do you keep physical intimacy intimate as well as physical?

Some couples find the matter of having children settled by a happily accidental pregnancy, but deciding to put away the pills and condoms and do what sex was evolutionarily designed to do – make a new person – can be a psychological leap. Regular sex without the worry about getting pregnant can be fun, but it can bring certain pressures, too.

Is tonight the night?

If you're tracking ovulation cycles and trying not to miss monthly windows of opportunity, sex can start to feel a bit mechanical. About 84 in every 100 couples conceive within a year, which is not exactly guaranteed – so it's possible you'll also be feeling anxious.

Some experts advise having as much sex as possible to maximize your chances, while others advise that you save sex for around ovulation time. With no real consensus, your best

bet is almost certainly to do whatever appeals most. Even if you do decide to save sex for ovulation, there's no reason not to have sensuous cuddles and fooling around at other times. You're taking this on together, so the closer you are emotionally, the better.

Can't get in the mood?

Trying for a baby may sound like a stress-free excuse for enthusiastic sex all the time – but don't feel guilty if that isn't the case. Everyone's natural drive is different, and stage fright can happen to the best of us.

If you find that nerves are making you freeze up, the best thing to do for both your sakes is to lower the expectations. Women, for instance, may find that the pressure interferes with their bodies' natural lubrication: rather than feeling inadequate, buy some non-spermicidal lubricant. Men, meanwhile, may find it more difficult for them to rise to the occasion: if that's the case, talk about introducing some erotica just for the

moment, to help things along – by bringing in a bit of extra stimulation or just helping you have a giggle about the whole business.

When you're watching the calendar every month it's easy to get drawn into a cycle of hope and disappointment. It's easier said than done, but your best bet is to reduce expectations and try to see the funny side. The sex doesn't have to be earth-shattering to create a baby, but if you can keep working together, supporting each other in insecure moments, and going as easy on yourself as you can, that's still pretty good lovemaking.

> Many couples are not aware that chance plays a big role in getting pregnant ... so finding out that it isn't happening can be a shock.
>
> **Geraldine Hartshorne**
> Warwick Medical School

WHAT ARE THE ODDS?

Most couples conceive within a year of having regular sex with no contraception. Women can have healthy babies well into their forties, but age does have an effect on fertility. A UK study in 2012 shows that the longer we've been trying, the more likely infertility is an issue and the less likely we'll conceive within the next month:

Age	Number of months trying to get pregnant and probability of conception within the next month					
	3 months	6 months	9 months	12 months	24 months	36 months
25	18%	15%	12%	10%	6%	3%
30	16%	13%	11%	9%	4%	2%
35	12%	9%	7%	6%	2%	1%
40	7%	5%	4%	3%	1%	0.5%

Coping with infertility

Few things are as painful as the experience of a couple who want to have a baby and find, or fear, that they can't. That pain is real and shouldn't be brushed off: a study in the *Indian Journal of Community Psychology*, for instance, found in 2010 that involuntarily childless people (particularly women) suffered more anxiety and depression than couples with children.

Medical intervention such as IVF can sometimes help, but doesn't always work, which brings its own difficulties. Sex can start to suffer after the physical and emotional ordeal of treatment: a 2007 study by Judith C. Daniluk and Elizabeth Tench at the University of British Columbia followed the progress of 38 couples for 33 months after unsuccessful fertility treatment and found that while their self-esteem began to recover, their sex life tended to diminish unless they had good social and emotional support (though the couples who adopted tended to fare better).

Even people whose treatment has been successful don't always feel completely recovered. A 2004 study in Sweden, for instance, found that while parents whose children were conceived by IVF faced similar parenting stresses to those who conceived naturally, the negative feelings they experienced towards their own fertility were not easily shaken off.

In such circumstances, partners will be coping with considerable emotional distress. It may very well affect them differently, calling for extra tolerance and empathy on both sides at a time when just coping with their own feelings may be all each partner feels up to. Get as much support as you possibly can, consider counselling, and try to be patient with each other and with yourselves.

1 in 7

Fertility problems affect one in seven couples in the UK.

15–25%

The odds of **getting pregnant** in any given month are roughly 15–25 per cent (subject to factors like age, health, and how often you have sex).

The best time to get pregnant is **a day or so either side of ovulation** – on average, **around day 14** of the cycle, but this varies from woman to woman.

BABY ON THE WAY
STAYING SEXUAL DURING PREGNANCY

Sexual relationships make for pregnancy – but does pregnancy have to unmake a sexual relationship? Not necessarily. Adaptability can get you through those 40-odd weeks without having to resort to celibacy.

During pregnancy, our bodies, minds, and hearts are all in turmoil. How do you hang on to the connection that led to this pregnancy in the first place – including the physical connection?

For some couples, especially those who've always been careful about contraception, pregnancy can be tremendously freeing: for once in your lives, you can have sex without worrying about unwanted pregnancy. For others, though, it can be a time of sex-inhibiting anxiety – not least anxiety about the baby.

> This is a time when you'll need plenty of communication and mutual empathy.

Will we hurt the baby?
It's generally agreed that, in most pregnancies, sex is perfectly safe. The uterus is a tough muscle – a little love-making is not going to disturb it – and the baby is safely cushioned inside the amniotic fluid.

For the sake of caution, though, you might have a chat with the doctor to set your mind at ease, especially if you have any medical conditions that could cause complications. Don't be embarrassed: a good doctor should support your right to enjoy yourselves.

Hormonal changes
Pregnancy floods the body with oestrogen and progesterone, and depending on the individual and the moment, you might feel sick and crampy, or like a tigress who can't wait to pounce on her partner. Your partner may feel a little overwhelmed by these changes: hormones can

whip up our moods, and both of you may sometimes struggle to keep up. It's good to be mutually considerate in any situation, but the woman may be feeling extra vulnerable and deserves some extra patience.

On the male side, it's worth noting that semen contains small quantities of prostaglandin – the same hormone that doctors use in pessaries and gels to induce overdue labour. This may sound alarming – talk to your doctor if you're not sure – but it's highly unlikely to have any effect on a cervix that isn't already ripe. It is, though, the reason why couples sometimes have a lot of sex late in pregnancy, in the hopes of getting labour started. By that time, the woman will feel pretty enormous and barely mobile: comfortable positions and low expectations are the most important things here.

Beautiful bump?
For some women, a blooming bump makes them feel sexier than ever, while others feel fat, frumpy, and undesirable. This is a time when you'll need plenty of communication and mutual empathy, especially as men also have differing feelings when it comes to pregnancy – some find it

gorgeously feminine, some feel it's nature's "no entry" sign, and some feel it's somehow impolite to get into the baby's space. If it's putting the man off his stroke, don't forget there are many ways of pleasing each other that don't involve penetrative sex. After all, if variety is the spice of life, you might as well seize the chance.

Physical changes

Breasts tend to swell and become more sensitive or tender, and sometimes leak milk as the baby approaches full term (which some men find alarming and some irresistible); there's an increased flow of blood to the whole genital area, which again can increase sensitivity; some positions can be untenable, as the upward-pressing womb causes heartburn; the pelvic ligaments can loosen in the last weeks, making walking painful. In short, the pregnant body is unpredictable and can surprise its owner in all sorts of ways, some of which are great for sex and some of which are disastrous.

> Sex is physically intimate, but physical intimacy goes beyond sex.

An open mind and imagination are your best friends while facing the next nine months. There may be times when the male partner needs to take some cold showers or confine his activity to sex with himself, but that needn't exclude the woman's company. Sex is physically intimate, but physical intimacy goes beyond sex, so try to have as much of the non-sexual kind as you can.

🔍 BABY BRAIN?

Numerous studies confirm that some women experience "baby brain", or short-term memory loss during pregnancy: for some pregnant women, it can sometimes be surprisingly hard to recall what has just happened. Psychologist Laura Glynn of Chapman University suggests that this helps a mother to focus on the needs of her unborn child. Whatever the reason, a partner needs to strike a delicate balance between respecting mum's intelligence and accepting her scattiness.

Help! What have we done?

Even couples who have planned a pregnancy can feel panicky once it goes from a plan to a reality. That's actually a good sign, showing you're responsible parents taking it seriously – but if the panic temporarily puts you off your stride, try other forms of intimacy so that you don't miss out.

Above all, communicate. If this is your first pregnancy, you may both feel at sea. How it will affect both of you physically and emotionally is impossible to predict. Don't rely on guesswork: you're in new territory now, so make a point of asking each other how you're feeling.

When the baby arrives, don't feel guilty if you feel overwhelmed at having to learn so many new skills on so little sleep – or if your love for your baby feels less like instant adoration, more like slow-growing affection. One in 10 mothers suffers post-natal depression, but all partners should be extra aware of a woman's wellbeing once the pregnancy is over. Keep communicating, and have faith you'll come through this together.

🔍 RELAXED OR PANICKED?

The psychological effects of pregnancy vary – to help each other cope, some common experiences to watch for:

In the first trimester,

- Anxiety about the baby's wellbeing: as miscarriage is most likely in the early weeks, it's easy to worry.
- Tension can exacerbate morning sickness, which is stressful in itself.
- Emotional highs/lows: a woman's hormones play a part, but so does her disposition and support system.
- Fatigue and low energy: a partner will need to let the woman be the judge of how much rest she needs.

In the second trimester,

- The feeling of physical wellbeing increases, which helps the mood. Women who were worried about miscarriage may also start to relax as the baby's chances improve.
- As bloodflow to the pelvic region increases, a woman may feel more tingly and erotic.
- Some women feel socially excluded, "fat", unattractive, vulnerable – and more in need of a protective partner.
- Bonding with the baby becomes easier as it starts to move noticably.

In the third trimester,

- With labour drawing near, anxiety is only natural. Late-term pregnancy can be especially uncomfortable.
- Work stress can increase as you try to get ready for parental leave.

Partners, especially men, can feel confused, out of things, and – in their role as protector – unable to talk freely. A good support network can be crucial.

A UNITED FRONT

HOW TO SHARE PARENTING WITHOUT GOING CRAZY

Few things put a relationship between parents under more strain than a clash of values over how to handle your children. How can you keep yourselves harmonious when the kids act up?

It's Friday night: it's been a long week, you're exhausted, your children come home from school yelling and misbehaving … and if your partner undermines your discipline, you know there'll be a meltdown. How to avoid the drama?

 STAY ATTACHED

Your attachment style may come into play when you parent: anxious people are afraid of abandonment and can overreact to naughtiness or be overly protective, while avoidant people are uncomfortable with extreme emotion and can be unsympathetic or dismissive when the kids need patience. We know adults use their romantic partners as a safe haven (see pages 30–31): when your children trigger your stress systems, remember your attachment style and ask your partner to help you get things settled. Parenting is often difficult, so it's okay to need extra help: guidance from other parents can be helpful, and supportive couples can care for each other while caring for their children.

Q **THINK AHEAD**

The couples least likely to fall out of love post-baby, according to research published in the *Journal of Family Psychology* in 2009, are those who were happiest beforehand – but also those whose children were planned, not accidental. Contraception can be a nuisance short term, but long term the odds favour couples who have conceived by design.

SORT OUT YOUR ISSUES

No one gets through children without a few bumps, and children can be surprisingly effective at bringing up painful memories – through no fault of their own, of course. You may find it helpful to sort your parenting needs (yes, parents have needs too) into two categories: things that bother you because they go against what you consider reasonable rules for any child to follow, and things that bother you because of personal associations.

Suppose, for instance, you had a bullying brother who used to beat you up when you were kids: your issues when you see your own children play-fighting may look something like the diagram below.

Both circles are important: families have to live with each other, after all. Sit down with your partner and work out what your "always unacceptable" and "personal issues" are, so that when you're under stress you can help each other stay fair. This is a time when a good partner can help you to be your best self.

RULES VERSUS NEEDS
When your rules and your personal issues overlap, it can be easy to lose it with your children. This is when it's most valuable to have your partner's guidance on how much discipline is enough.

GET IT STRAIGHT

The moment your children are climbing the walls is not the moment to make important decisions about discipline: what you need to do is communicate in advance. Try making two different lists.

1 **House rules.** What's acceptable and what's not. (For instance: no violence, use a nice voice, respect one another's things...). Keep it simple, as too many complex rules confuse children. And remember, once you've made the rules, you'll have to stick to them yourselves. If you find your partner undermines your decisions, revisit the rules when your children are not around.

2 **Consequences.** Improvising in the heat of the moment is a bad idea. Agree what you consider to be a fair penalty and what kinds of behaviour should warrant it.

Children need consistency, but this will also give you more sense of control: one reason why parents overreact to bad behaviour and take it out on each other is that it's disempowering to feel unable to cope with a crisis. Once you and your partner have agreed rules that reflect both your values, you've built support for each other into the life of the household.

OPENING OLD WOUNDS

If you've had a rough childhood yourself, it can be difficult to be the parent you want to be: even if you vowed you'd never take it out on your children, in the moment they're driving you crazy, you can regress to old bad habits. The good news is that, according to a 2013 study published in the *Journal of Adolescent Health*, positive communication and warmth from your partner can be very effective at helping you break the cycle.

If you know you didn't see the ideal model in your parents, your partner is your best ally. Agree a signal for your partner to tell you, "You're losing it, step back and let me handle this", and look to them to be your coach when things get difficult.

On the other hand, if you feel confident about your parenting but your partner has issues, then it's most effective to emphasize that you respect them for their efforts even when they do make mistakes. Breaking abusive cycles is hard and heroic work, and it's best to do it as a heroic couple fighting the same demon together.

Things that are always unacceptable: Physical tussles can get out of hand and end in hurting each other or breaking something.

My kids' play-fighting makes me nervous.

Things that are my own personal issues: The sight of children in a tussle brings up horrible memories from my own childhood.

PARENTS' DATE NIGHT

HAVING SOME FUN IN THE FEW SPARE MOMENTS

If you know the joy of parenthood, you'll know the rarity value that a night alone together can have. After all the effort and fatigue, how do you actually manage to enjoy yourselves once you get there?

Even the best parents in the world need some time alone just as a couple, but it can be hard to switch from parents to dating couple in the short space of time available. What's the solution?

Help yourselves along

Remember those early days of your romance when you stayed up all night talking? Talking to each other is very nice even if you have heard all each other's stories by now. These days, you may have to be a little more organized – a skill you've been cultivating ever since you became parents. You'll have to arrange babysitters in advance, for example, or you won't be able to go out.

While you're planning the date in advance, you can plan some topics of conversation as well. Never mind spontaneity: while the children are still young, any kind of romantic connection is an accomplishment. Whatever your interests, think about something you'd find fun to discuss with your partner and then save the discussion for date night. If the conversation takes off from there, wonderful, but if that's all you've got to talk about for a while, at least you've definitely got a topic.

Don't go overboard

To quote French playwright and philosopher Voltaire, "The perfect is

> Making someone a cup of tea ... is very important to people. Those little gestures can be as important as profound conversation.
>
> **Lynn Jamieson**
> Sociology professor,
> Univerity of Edinburgh

WHAT ARE YOUR GOALS?

Your date night is so precious, it's understandable if you have high expectations of making it truly meaningful. It's usually best, though, to keep your goals concrete rather than abstract. Research conducted at Harvard Business School and published in the *Journal of Experimental Psychology* found that setting out to make someone smile more, for example, led to greater satisfaction than something big and vague such as "Make someone happy". The simpler the goal, the more likely the outcome will match your expectations and the more rewarding that will feel.

the enemy of the good". You may well feel that two weeks on a tropical beach would just about do it in terms of rest and reconnection – but you may have to settle for less. Children strain resources – time, money, and energy, to name but a few. If you pressure yourselves into stretching those resources even further on big-ticket treats, you'll probably be too worried to feel romantic.

If money's tight, you don't even have to go to a fancy restaurant: pick a local bar or coffee shop, spin out a single drink, or pack sandwiches for a walk in the park. If you can't manage a babysitter, stay in and switch the TV firmly off: try a board game that encourages easy conversation, or a game that involves imaginative fooling around, like charades.

Getting any time to yourselves when there are small people about can be difficult, but don't short-change yourselves: you have to work together as a

CAN'T KEEP YOUR EYES OPEN?

Parents with young children can be particularly exhausted. Here are some tips for having a good date despite the fatigue:

✔ **Schedule a daytime date.** Find a babysitter who's willing to take the kids on a weekend lunchtime or afternoon and then go out and enjoy yourselves for a couple of hours before you're completely worn out.

✔ **Camp out in your bedroom.** Remember those sleepovers or campfires of your youth, where you told ghost stories and dirty jokes? They were fun, weren't they? As long as there's no child in your bed, you can always take your date there and try to scare and/or titillate each other.

✔ **Get in the water.** There's nothing like a proper soak to ease a battered body. If your local leisure centre has a hydrotherapy or spa pool, book a session there for the two of you. If not, just go to your local pool when there's a free swim and chill out in the shallow end, letting your limbs float and having a soothing conversation.

family, and the work is a lot more rewarding when you feel like a connected couple rather than a business partnership. The day will come when you do have more time again, but until then, plan your own fun with the same care you'd plan time with your kids: if anyone deserves it, you do.

STUCK FOR A BABYSITTER?

If you have friends from antenatal class, or your children have friends from playgroup, nursery, or school, these fellow parents are your new best buddies. Approach them and propose to exchange "play dates" at each other's houses. If the children settle in, then you can take turns to supervise play dates and go out.

In effect you're paying the sitter in kind rather than with money. Added to that, your children will be all the better entertained by having their friends round when it's your turn to have a play date. (Assuming their friends aren't awful – check before you commit!) You win either way, and you get to go on date nights.

HIT THE OPEN ROAD

If there's really nowhere nice within reach, you've got to get back in an hour, and you have a car, then go for a quiet drive. You may not be able to go for a massive road trip, but think of the advantages: it's private, there's just the two of you, you get to pick the music, and you have a roof over your heads. Pack some snacks if you like, and just tootle along talking.

SEE YOU AT SEX O'CLOCK
MAKING TIME FOR SEX

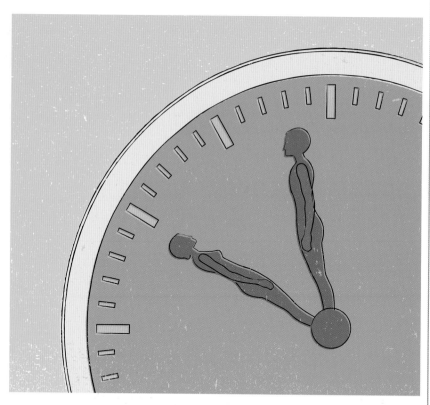

When family responsibilities take up so much of your time and energy, spontaneous sex may appear to be off the cards – but that doesn't have to mean your sex life has to come to an end.

When children are young, parents know from experience that if anything's going to happen, it pretty much has to be planned in advance. If everything else is scheduled, then, why not sex? It may sound odd to put sex on the to-do list as if it's a chore, but the important fact is this: just because you know it's planned in advance doesn't mean the sex itself is going to be boring.

It's easy to assume that we have sex because we want to, but actually it can go the other way as well: motivation can follow on from action. This isn't just true of sex: consider, for instance, how often you find yourself tidying the whole living room because you spotted a stray toy, started picking things up, and then decided you might as well carry on?

If you and your partner start kissing and cuddling, there's a good chance you'll start to get excited even if you weren't to begin with. Of course, this is no justification for forcing the issue against your partner's will: mutual consent is the only foundation for a healthy relationship. But given an atmosphere of trust, trying to get into it even if you don't expect much can be surprisingly effective.

Putting the horse before the cart
To cite American marriage counsellor Michele Weiner-Davis, "I wish I had a

> Motivation does not come first, action does! You have to prime the pump.
>
> **David D. Burns, M.D.**
> Professor of psychiatry and behavioural sciences, and author of *Feeling Good*

THE COMPLEX CYCLE OF FEMALE DESIRE

According to Rosemary Basson, clinical professor of psychiatry and director of sexual medicine at the University of British Columbia, women's experience of desire and sexuality isn't necessarily a straightforward progression from desire to orgasm. Instead, the cycle can begin at a number of different points – especially if you're a woman in a long-term relationship – and only some of them begin with physical lust. If you're not sure you feel up to sex just now, think about where on the cycle you might like to begin and see if that makes sex look more approachable. You have more options than you might expect.

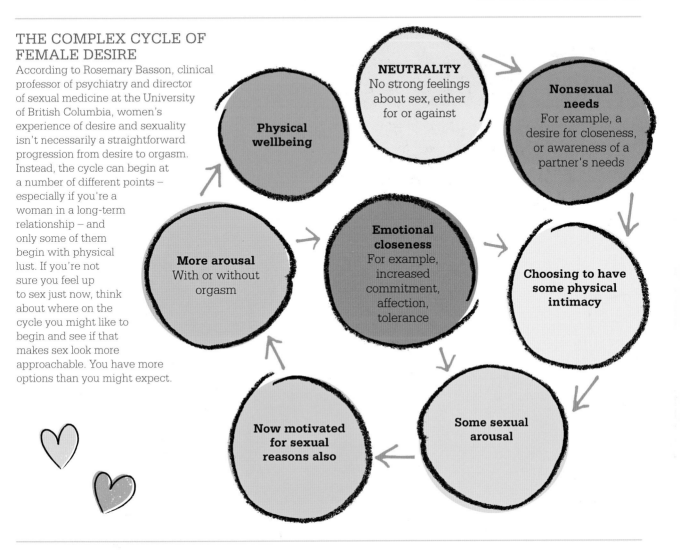

dollar for each time someone in my practice said … 'I wasn't in the mood … but once we got into it, I had a really good time!'" Sometimes we just have to get started before we feel like starting. Weiner-Davis bases this advice on the work of Rosemary Basson at the University of British Columbia. Sexual desire is generally categorized as four stages – desire, arousal, orgasm, and resolution – but Basson argues that arousal and desire are often reversed (see above), and that for women in particular, sexual desire is often responsive rather than spontaneous: being approached by a partner or starting to do sexual things creates arousal, which in turn creates the desire for sex.

Sexuality and physical affection are a crucial part of how we communicate our romantic feelings towards each other. Certainly there are phases of life where we're exhausted, busy, and not really in the mood – but if you try being a little more strategic than usual, your body might just decide it's capable of more than you think. A little sensuous time out together might be just what you need.

> Committed sex is premeditated sex. It's willful, it's intentional: it's focus and presence.
>
> **Esther Perel**
> Psychotherapist and author of *Mating In Captivity: Unlocking Erotic Intelligence*

KEEPING THE SPARK

BURNING LONG AND BURNING BRIGHT

If we're lucky enough to find lifelong love, how do we stay out of a rut and keep the relationship romantic? Romantic love and emotional closeness don't have to become routine even if they are familiar.

There can come a day when you and your partner run out of things to do. You're retired or your careers are stable; your children, if you have any, are now old enough to take care of themselves. What now? How do you stay excited about each other now everything's calmed down?

Staying in love

Couples can stay in love for decades, even if they are completely used to each other. A study led by Bianca Acevedo and Arthur Aron of Stony Brook University, for instance, examined couples who had been married for an average of 21 years and claimed to still be madly in love. When they were placed in an fMRI scanner, being shown pictures of their beloved did indeed light up the same dopamine-rich regions of their brain associated with the early stages of a romance. But they were also less obsessive than new couples, and the regions of their brains associated with liking and attachment lit up too – neurologically speaking, they had the best of all worlds. They could think straight but were deeply in love and genuinely fond of their partners all at once. Long-burning romances do empirically happen.

🔍 GOOD FOR YOUR HEALTH

Marriage, if it lasts, turns out to be good for you. In 2009, an international study led by clinical psychologist Kate Scott across 15 countries and 34,493 people reported that married people were at reduced risk of depression, anxiety, and substance abuse. A supportive partner might literally lengthen your life.

🔍 HOW DO YOU DO IT?

When Stony Brook psychologist Daniel O'Leary and colleagues studied long-term couples still passionately in love, they found:

1 They had positive thoughts about each other. They dwelled on each other's good points.

2 They thought about each other when apart.

3 They didn't mentally multi-task. When they were thinking about each other, the image of their beloved held their full attention.

4 They had fun sharing new and challenging activities, whether physical or mental. O'Leary found this was particularly helpful for men: sharing a new experience refreshes your feelings for the person you share it with.

5 They spent time together. Even pottering around doing chores together was bonding.

6 They were physically affectionate. Hugs, pats, and kisses on the cheek kept the spark.

7 They were physically attracted to each other. The couples said they felt warm and tingly when their partners touched them.

8 They kept a sexual spark. It's a two-way street – we're more likely to have sex with someone we love – but showing affection and enjoying physical contact helps the spark.

9 They were happy people – both happily in love and happy about life in general. For women in particular, a general sense of wellbeing helped the romance.

10 They wanted to know where the other one was at all times. They didn't tip over into stalking, but they did want to know what was going on with each other, especially the men.

11 They thought about each other a lot. The women, in particular, could be a bit obsessive about their partners.

12 They were enthusiastic people. Getting fired up about life helped them get fired up about each other, particularly the men.

In short, staying curious, passionate, cheerful, and kind can be the best recipe for a happy long-term relationship – and in turn, a happy relationship can help us to stay cheerful and kind.

🔍 PEACE AND LOVE

A major difference between new and established romance shows up in the opioid- and serotonin-rich regions of the brain. In new couples, not much is happening there, but in long-established ones, fMRI scans show that the presence of a partner makes the regions very active. Since those regions are associated with regulating anxiety and pain, long-standing romances bring a feeling of tranquility: the brain is on a nice, mild high, which makes you feel calm and contented.

Looking ahead

If you're single, does it help to read about long-term goals? Well, yes: if you want a relationship that will last, then scoping out the options with the knowledge that you need someone who'll be right for you through all the changes life brings can help you to identify the good ones. And if you've already picked out someone who looks like a good prospect, it still helps to look ahead.

Love isn't the answer to everything and those who expect it to be tend to have the least fulfilling love lives. What love can be, if you're lucky and you work at it, is a solid base from which you can tackle everything positively, creatively, and confidently.

At its best, a romantic relationship isn't something that turns you into a new, better person: it's something that, as the years go on, supports you as you continue to grow into a psychologically healthier, happier, and more authentic version of the person you always were – as does love of any kind, whether you are in love or not.

As you search for, consider, date, and fall in and out of love with potential partners, stay true to your best self and keep your eyes open for the person who will make it not harder but easier to be that person.

INDEX

Page numbers in **bold** refer to main entries.